MARINE
DIESEL ENGINES
CARE & MAINTENANCE

MARINE DIESEL ENGINES
CARE & MAINTENANCE

PETER CAPLEN

THE CROWOOD PRESS

First published in 2010 by
The Crowood Press Ltd
Ramsbury, Marlborough
Wiltshire SN8 2HR

www.crowood.com

British Library Cataloguing-in-Publication Data
A catalogue record for this book is available from the British Library.

ISBN 978 1 84797 175 3

Disclaimer
The author and the publisher do not accept any responsibility in any manner whatsoever for any error or omission, or any loss, damage, injury, adverse outcome or liability of any kind incurred as a result of the use of any of the information contained in this book, or reliance upon it.

Dedication
With love to 'Mumsie', still helping the old folks while spending the inheritance!

Originated by The Manila Typesetting Company

Printed and bound in India by Replika Press Ltd

Contents

Introduction

Despite recent changes in fuel taxation for privately owned boats, the diesel engine is still by far the most popular form of propulsive power for boats of all sizes, both power and sail. Although the loss of some taxation benefits has caused a rise in the price of diesel so it approaches that of petrol, there can be no doubt that diesel is still the best choice for boats. Gas oil, or 'red diesel', is the standard fuel for marine diesel engines; it is far less flammable than petrol, which is why it is unheard of for a diesel-powered craft to suffer from a fuel tank explosion – something which cannot be said of petrol-engined craft, as the number of incidents, although fairly low, is depressingly regular.

Diesel engines are also twice as reliable as the petrol engine – in theory at least – because they have no electrical ignition system, which in the marine environment is always prone to suffer from the effects of the damp surroundings. However, in the last ten years or so electronically controlled diesels have to some extent lost this advantage. Then again, the sealed computer-based electronic systems used for controlling diesel engines are much less exposed than the petrol engine ignition system. The high levels of reliability of modern electronics mean that a complete breakdown is very unlikely, and this, coupled with the high efficiency and fuel economy of modern common-rail diesels, still gives the diesel engine a big economy edge over the petrol version.

These virtues make the diesel engine the favoured choice of the serious boat owner, who regards safety and reliability of paramount importance. Also to be considered is the fact that the economy of the diesel engine allows a vessel with a given fuel tank capacity to travel that much further when powered by diesel rather than petrol.

The easy availability of gas oil from boat yards and marinas makes refuelling more convenient; many yards are unable to stock petrol due to the stringent regulations covering the storage of petrol, which requires the additional heavy expense of installing underground tanks. The only area of the UK where petrol is readily available at nearly all marinas is the south coast, and in this area there are many more petrol-powered boats than in other areas. Moreover the fact that gas oil is still somewhat cheaper than petrol despite the loss in 2008 of the derogation allowing non-road diesel fuel to be taxed at a lower rate means that motor boating can still be enjoyed on a reasonable budget without too many worries about how wide the throttles are opened!

Many boat owners are still unfamiliar with the workings of the diesel engine, although with the prevalence of high efficiency diesels now commonly being used in cars, their mysteries are less puzzling. Anyone with a basic working knowledge of petrol engines will have a good basis for understanding the diesel, as there is little real difference between the two apart from the fuel system and the lack of an electrical ignition system. The mechanics of the diesel engine are basically identical to that of the petrol engine, and once the differences in fuelling are understood, they should not present any problems to the enthusiastic DIY owner.

This book explains everything the beginner needs to know to keep their boat's diesel engines in good order, how to rectify simple faults, and how to save a great deal of cash on annual service costs. It will also be of benefit to the more knowledgeable owner who wants to fill in the gaps in their knowledge. It covers all the basic maintenance procedures, and also explains the workings of power-boosting equipment such as turbochargers, superchargers and intercoolers, and the way different types of marine cooling systems operate.

While there is a huge selection of practical material there is also plenty of detail about the history and development of the diesel engine. Hopefully this will give the owner a much better insight into (and interest in) their power unit than a straightforward workshop manual could provide. Unlike a workshop manual that explains no more than how to perform certain tasks, this book attempts to provide a basic understanding of the workings of the diesel engine; furthermore, while offering step-by-step instruction on practical maintenance procedures, it also explains exactly why each job is required.

Several sections concentrate on areas that many owners may not have considered of great importance. Fuel tanks are a case in point. Give a diesel engine a supply of clean, air-free fuel and even if it is almost totally 'clapped out' it will probably still run; but introduce dirt or air into the fuel, and even a new engine will soon stop in protest. A clean fuel supply is the key to reliable running. Therefore, although these items may be unglamorous and unpleasant to deal with,

they will ultimately reward the owner with a trouble-free season's boating.

The largest chapters necessarily concentrate on the fuel, cooling and electrical systems, as these are where problems are most likely to occur. The cooling system will cause problems if it is not properly cleaned and maintained; in the worst case scenario the engine will overheat to the point of seizure, so it is most important to keep the cooling system in good order, yet this does not require any great degree of skill. Similarly some basic maintenance of the electrical system will ensure the engine starts when the key is turned, and continues running and charging the batteries until it is switched off.

Much of the practical content of this book is drawn from a long experience of keeping ailing diesel engines running on a minimal budget and with the minimum of facilities. This can be part of the pleasure of owning a vessel with inboard power, and for those who must work to a tight budget it is an almost essential skill!

It is a fact that a job completed by the owner, once the necessary knowledge has been acquired, will be of a higher standard than that performed by a service agent or boatyard as the owner knows only too well that if problems arise at sea it will be up to him alone to find the remedy, and that if a job is performed properly in the first place a problem will not arise later.

However, regardless of the financial considerations of the reader and whether or not they choose to have their annual maintenance performed professionally, self-sufficiency at sea and the ability to solve minor engine problems without having to alert the lifeboat is a part of good seamanship, and being able to rectify minor breakdowns should be a matter of pride. Your engine is your lifeline, and it is as well always to remember that the welfare state ends at the sea wall!

CHAPTER 1

A Brief History of Diesel Engine Development

Although the early development of the diesel engine is naturally connected with the name Rudolf Diesel, like other complex machinery its progress was a combination of the work of many separate individuals. While Rudolf Diesel was a first class engineer in his own right, serving his basic engineering apprenticeship in various engineering fields, it was without doubt his final designs and prototypes that formed the first true diesel engines as we know them today.

Due to the lack of effective communications in the nineteenth century there was little chance of liaison between engineers in different countries. Thus engineers working alone were designing and constructing experimental engines on similar lines, without any knowledge of anyone else's advances.

INTERNAL COMBUSTION: THE WAY FORWARDS

The diesel engine was conceived along with the petrol engine over a period of years as an answer to the horrendous inefficiency of the steam engine, which was at best only about 10 per cent fuel efficient, wasting 90 per cent of the fuel energy being used. Furthermore the development of the steam engine had reached its peak, and no more significant improvements in fuel efficiency would be possible. It was well known that internal combustion was the way forwards, rather than the external combustion of the steam engine. Internal combustion would immediately save the loss of heat from which the steam engine suffered when transferring heat energy from the boiler to the cylinder.

During the early days the most conveniently available fuel source for stationary engines was town gas, and it was with this fuel that early experiments with internal combustion engines were conducted. The principle of the four-stroke cycle for internal combustion had been furnished by Frenchman Alphonse Beau de Rochas in 1862, while at the same time in Germany Nikolaus August Otto, unaware of the work of de Rochas, actually built a four-stroke engine; for many reasons this could not be made to run smoothly, but although it did actually manage to run, the idea was shelved.

In 1876, after further research, Otto developed an improved version of the four-stroke engine. One of the problems with early designs was the harsh clattering noise that the piston made as it reached the top of its stroke. To try to overcome this, the piston was allowed to travel further up the bore and thus increase the air pressure within to act as a damper for the piston before ignition. This development did indeed dramatically cut the mechanical noise of the engine, but more importantly it was found that the efficiency of the engine was hugely improved. At this point Otto patented the four-stroke cycle in Germany, and in fact it is still occasionally known as the 'Otto' cycle, especially by older engineers with more traditional apprentice training.

The next challenge was to free the engine from the gas pipe supplying it with fuel! Powdered coal was tried unsuccessfully, which led to the idea of using liquefied fuel. The first engines were petrol-fuelled and utilized crude carburettors and glowing platinum igniters. After much experimentation a low voltage electric spark was used for the ignition system, and the forerunner of today's spark plug was born – an idea which incidentally had been tried in Italy some twenty years previously!

RUDOLF DIESEL

As a young engineer Rudolf Diesel began his career with Sulzer of Switzerland building ice-making machines. His first attempts at engine development were in the form of an improved type of steam engine but using ammonia rather than water vapour as the power source; this was not a success, however. He had followed with fascination the developments being made in the field of internal combustion, and having the benefit of a first class education and a sound understanding of thermodynamics, he turned his attention to his own theories of internal combustion.

At this stage in the development process fairly crude internal combustion engines were being produced, for use in factories to power machinery, and also modified for use as marine engines, particularly in fishing boats. Although all these machines tended to be low revving and produced relatively low power, they were vastly more fuel efficient than the steam engine.

Yorkshireman Herbert Akroyd Stuart designed a 'hot bulb' engine which was also known as a 'semi-diesel'. It operated using the four-stroke cycle, with fuel sprayed into the combustion chamber at the top of the compression stroke. This fuel was ignited by a glowing hot metal bulb (as the name implies), which had to be preheated with a blow lamp for eight minutes before the engine could be started. Once it was running the heat of combustion maintained the temperature of the bulb so that the engine ran continuously. Although this engine was low powered and very unsophisticated it was built in the thousands for industrial and marine use, where in both cases it could be relied upon to give a long and reliable life.

Diesel's designs were largely aimed at attaining better fuel efficiency, with the ultimate goal of 100 per cent – which as a realist he knew could not be achieved. He turned his attention back to the many lessons he had learned in his early years, and decided that for maximum efficiency an engine would need to run at extremely high pressure. He was impressed with the theoretical efficiency of the four-stroke cycle, and set about designing a four-stroke engine with compression ignition, working with a cylinder pressure of $300kg/cm^2$. At that time these pressures were only found in volcanoes and bombs, so to give his design greater credibility he halved the maximum pressure to $150kg/cm^2$ – but even these figures were considered unattainable and were declined by manufacturers.

After reworking his figures he submitted a revised design with a working pressure of 44kg/cm^2, and this was accepted by Maschinenfabrik Augsburg (later to become the famous diesel engine manufacturers MAN), who agreed to build an experimental engine to see if the principle would work. With engineering standards at that time being fairly low due to the lack of high precision machinery, it took a great deal of time and experimentation just to achieve an effective seal within the cylinder; eventually, however, the test equipment was reading pressures on the compression stroke approaching the designed levels.

On the first ignition test in 1894 the glass pressure indicator on the cylinder head exploded due to the unexpectedly high pressure that rapidly developed within the cylinder when the fuel was sprayed in. The rest of the engine was undamaged, and the compression ignition principle was dramatically proven.

The engine was redesigned and could be coaxed into life for short periods of time; although accompanied by violent detonations and clouds of smoke, it proved that a compression ignition engine could work. From then on it was a case of trial and error to improve on the original design.

Over the years there were various improvements, each offering greater fuel efficiency, but the overriding problem was the fuel injection system, which in early engines used an air blast system requiring a compressor to supply the pressurized air. It was not until the end of World War I that a satisfactory airless injection system was perfected and put into production.

INDIRECT INJECTION

During the period between the first successful running of Rudolph Diesel's first

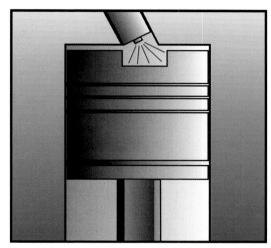

A simplified view of direct diesel injection.

engine and the end of World War I there was also progress made with pre-combustion chamber design, now known as indirect injection. This was developed by another engineer, Prosper l'Orange, along with an airless injection system which improved efficiency by removing the need for the auxiliary air compressor, which in itself cut down on power loss.

The pre-combustion chamber was a separate chamber in the cylinder head above the cylinder, into which air was forced by the rising of the piston during the compression stroke. This improved combustion and reduced detonation when the fuel was injected.

One of the benefits of the pre-combustion chamber design was found to be quieter combustion, although at a slight loss of thermal efficiency. It was an Englishman, Sir Harry Ricardo, who later perfected the system of indirect injection with his designs of swirl chamber; although this differed from the early pre-combustion chamber designs in that it was very much more sophisticated – air is induced

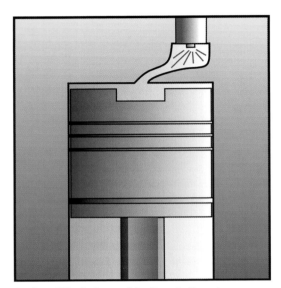

A simplified view of indirect diesel injection.

to swirl around the specially shaped chamber, thereby ensuring a good air/fuel mix and an even burn – the concept is basically very similar. Despite being designed in the 1930s, the Ricardo Comet Mark V combustion chamber was still one of the most popular designs of swirl chamber among engine manufacturers until more recent developments superseded them.

In 1925 another personality well known in the field of modern diesel fuel systems was making his name with the successful development of an improved fuel injection system following the experiences of other engineers. This was Robert Bosch, who had already enjoyed much success with his development of magneto spark ignition systems on petrol engines. Bosch fuel injection systems are today used on a wide range of modern engines, while the basic design is incorporated into the products of many other manufacturers.

THE TWO-STROKE ENGINE

In the quest for greater efficiency most early diesel engineers agreed that if a four-stroke engine was reasonably efficient, then surely a two-stroke with twice as many power strokes for the same revolutions would be doubly efficient. This was not the case, however, as the two-stroke required an external means of getting sufficient air into the cylinder for adequate combustion. This was provided in the form of a mechanical blower (or supercharger), which supplied air under pressure to the cylinder.

The two-stroke diesel became the accepted type for use in large power units, especially in ships, where the slow revving nature of the engine allowed plenty of time for the intake of air and the outflow of exhaust. Not so many small two-stroke diesels were produced, however, although such notable names as Foden and Detroit Allison were (and still are) very successful with their smaller two-strokes.

In fact the Detroit two-stroke diesel is still seen on many large American cruisers, although British owners tend to opt for four-stroke options simply because the two-stroke diesel is even more alien to them than the four-stroke. From the late 1920s diesel technology progressed at a steady pace, with further refinements being added and greater power being extracted from ever smaller and lighter engines.

DIESEL ENGINES FOR PLEASURE CRAFT

Although diesel engines advanced rapidly in the commercial and industrial field and became the standard power unit for

A Bedford 466 from the 1960s, producing a modest 140hp from a 7.6ltr block: a sought-after engine of its day.

ships and commercial craft of all types, it is only in the last forty years or so that it has come to be considered the standard powerplant for pleasure craft. After World War II the majority of smaller private vessels were petrol powered, and even when mass production of GRP craft began in the early sixties, the petrol engine was the favoured unit.

No doubt this was mainly due to the fact that petrol engines have always been cheaper to buy than diesels, and at the time petrol was a lot cheaper in real terms than it is now. The fact that small diesels were also significantly heavier and more bulky than their petrol equivalents probably also affected this decision. The significant number of cruising craft around today still fitted with their original petrol engines is evidence of this fact, although as they wear and spares run out, more and more are being converted to diesel.

In contrast the large number of US-built power boats now being sold in the UK has seen an increase in petrol power again, but this is simply because petrol is still cheap in the USA and there is little point in installing diesels at extra cost. Since the early 1970s, however, diesel progress has accelerated at an astonishing rate, and with the realization that oil supplies are not infinite, the quest for greater fuel economy naturally still leads to the diesel engine.

Improved fuel economy also brings with it increased overall efficiency, which leads to higher power-to-weight ratios. Thus in the last thirty years we have seen the change from petrol to diesel engines in leisure craft designed for serious cruising, and more recently even the high-speed express cruiser has gone over exclusively to diesel, with almost no loss of performance but a great improvement in fuel economy and lower fuel costs.

The number of diesel-powered cars on our roads has increased dramatically in the last two decades, and the staggering performance of many of them as they rush silently down the outside lane of the motorway is evidence enough of the progress made. This progress is now also being felt in the marine industry, with even small planing craft often being equipped with diesel powerplants.

One of the latest high-tech common-rail diesels from Volvo-Penta: the D4-300 producing 300hp from a 3.7ltr block.

As we have already seen, early diesel engines were very heavy and slow-revving, and compared to such old stalwarts of the small cruiser as the BMC 1.5 and 2.2, the later BL 1.8 and 2.5, the Ford 4D and the Bedford 220, all of which were popular with the DIY mariner in the not-too-distant past, they too in their turn are heavy, unsophisticated and slow-revving compared with the latest electronically controlled common-rail diesels now used in cars and trucks.

This new technology has found its way into the marine field, where it is not only high efficiency and low fuel consumption that is gained, but the clouds of smoke when starting on cold mornings are thankfully gone. Their compact size and high power-to-weight ratios indicate the advances that have been made in a relatively

short time, and make the comparatively low cost automotive diesel engine available for marinizing and installing in smaller and smaller vessels.

In the same manner the larger engines from manufacturers such as Volvo, Cummins and Caterpillar are all producing sophisticated power units with power-to-weight ratios that could only be dreamed of a few years ago. Furthermore, with the added power output comes greater fuel economy per horse-power, increased reliability and clean exhausts.

As the worldwide demand for diesel engines increases there are sure to be many more improvements to performance, fuel efficiency and exhaust emissions before engineers come to the same conclusion that they did with steam engines: that no further progress is possible!

CHAPTER 2

How the Diesel Engine Works

Before looking at the diesel engine in detail it is first worth considering the marine engine. The vast majority of modern marine engines on offer today begin their lives as basic vehicle or industrial units, and are then modified and adapted to suit the marine environment by the manufacturer.

With the high performance demanded from modern craft, the traditional marine engine with its low revs and heavy build designed to last for years cannot offer the power-to-weight ratio to satisfy this need. This is one reason why the lighter vehicle engine with high power-to-weight ratio has taken over the market; the other reason is cost. As we have seen, diesel technology is advancing all the time, with more power being extracted from smaller capacity units, which when carried to extremes inevitably leads to a shorter working life.

However, the modern high-performance diesel when in standard trim offers exceptional reliability and long life, and when fitted in a cruiser will almost certainly last the lifetime of the boat if maintained correctly at the appropriate intervals. What we know and accept as the marine diesel of today is far removed from the low-revving, heavy monster with its origins in the earliest of diesel engine designs. The

real marine engine is still in evidence in the vastly larger sizes used in ships, but the design of small high-performance engines, although greatly refined, would not be at all alien to Rudolf Diesel.

THE FOUR-STROKE DIESEL ENGINE

The four-stroke is by far the most popular of today's small marine diesel engines, although two-strokes are still available from at least one manufacturer. As we have already seen, the four-stroke cycle (at least in theoretical terms) has been around for well over a hundred years, and nothing has yet been developed to better it.

The cycle is identical for both petrol and diesel engines, and the name refers to the four strokes (two up and two down) that are needed to complete one power cycle, and which encompass two revolutions of the crankshaft. The basic four-stroke diesel engine comprises a heavily built block to withstand the high internal pressures that develop during the combustion process. This contains the cylinders that may be a combination of any number from one to twenty or more, although in the smaller

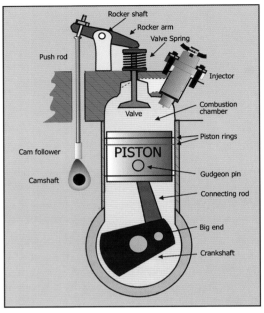

The internal workings of a simple diesel engine viewed from the front.

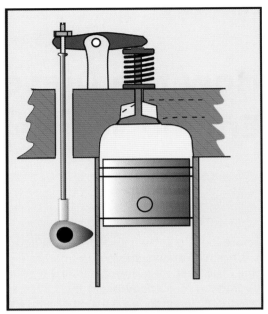

Detail of the closing of a valve (either inlet or exhaust).

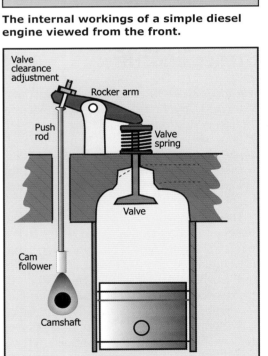

Detail of the opening of a valve (either inlet or exhaust).

A typical injector mounting arrangement.

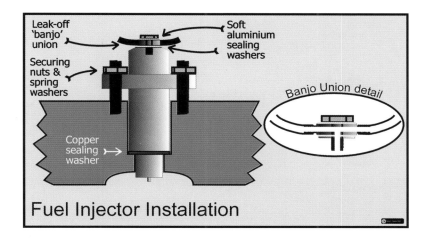

Leak-off 'banjo' union

Securing nuts & spring washers

Soft aluminium sealing washers

Banjo Union detail

Copper sealing washer

Fuel Injector Installation

sizes which we are dealing with, six would be a normal maximum and occasionally eight, probably in V formation.

The tops of the cylinders are sealed with a cylinder head; this is usually a single unit where the engine is an automotive derivative, but it can also be in the form of separate heads for each cylinder on larger units and in heavy-duty designs such as used by Gardner engines. The advantage of separate cylinder heads is that work can be performed on one cylinder without the need to disturb all the rest, as happens with engines with a single universal head.

The reason for using a single universal head on the majority of engines is, of course, cost. Within the cylinder head are passages to allow combustion air and exhaust gases to enter and leave the cylinder. The movement of these gases is controlled by inlet and exhaust valves, which open and close at predetermined times during the cycle, and which seal the cylinder during the compression and firing strokes.

The cylinder head also contains one injector for each cylinder, its purpose being to inject fuel at a high enough pressure to overcome the internal pressure within

Timing gears must be correctly aligned to ensure that the valves open and close and that fuel is injected at the correct moment.

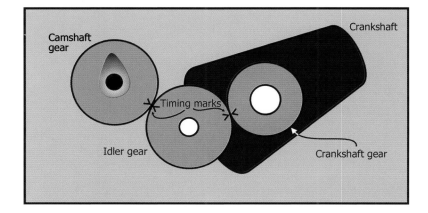

Camshaft gear

Crankshaft

Timing marks

Idler gear

Crankshaft gear

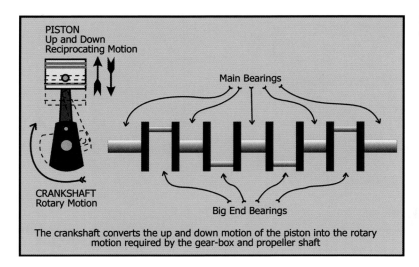

PISTON
Up and Down
Reciprocating Motion

Main Bearings

CRANKSHAFT
Rotary Motion

Big End Bearings

The crankshaft converts the up and down motion of the piston into the rotary
motion required by the gear-box and propeller shaft

Detail of a typical crankshaft.

the cylinder produced on the compression stroke.

The opening and closing of the inlet and exhaust valves is controlled by the camshaft, which is in turn driven via either a chain, gears or belt from the crankshaft. Within each cylinder is a piston which travels up and down. The gap between the cylinder walls and the piston is sealed with rings of cast iron, which are located in machined grooves in the piston body.

The rings are split at one point to allow them to expand outwards and maintain a constant pressure on the cylinder walls. There are usually three or four rings near the top of the piston and one near the bottom. The bottom ring and the lowest of the three or four top rings are usually oil-control (or scraper) rings, which instead of being solid iron are formed in a lattice arrangement. The grooves in which the oil-control rings are fitted have drillings through the piston body so that oil which has splashed or sprayed onto the cylinder walls for lubrication can be scraped off and returned to the sump via the drillings in the ring grooves.

When a piston and rings are assembled and fitted into a cylinder the rings are compressed by the cylinder walls and the split openings (known as gaps) are reduced to around 0.5 per cent of the cylinder diameter, which in a small engine would be in the region of 0.35mm. Nevertheless, it is very important to ensure that the gaps are staggered around the piston during assembly to ensure minimal cylinder pressure loss when running.

The lower part of the block below the cylinders supports the crankshaft in bearing carriers that are lined with replaceable white metal bearings. The number of carriers and bearings varies with engine make and design, but in general terms for maximum crankshaft support a 4-cylinder engine will have five bearings and a 6-cylinder engine will have seven. These would be known as a five-bearing and seven-bearing crank respectively. There are notable exceptions to this flexible rule, one of which is the old but very well known Perkins 4107 and its successor the 4108, which although being 4-cylinder engines use three-bearing cranks.

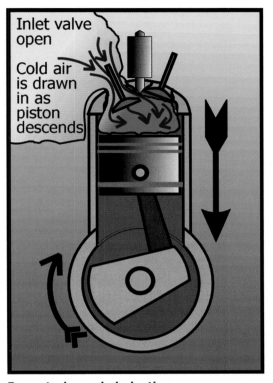

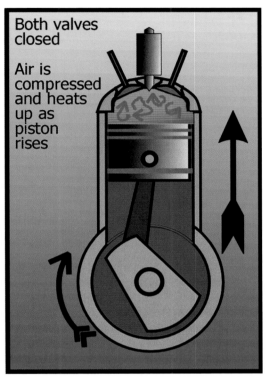

Four-stroke cycle induction.   **Four-stroke cycle compression.**

It is the job of the crankshaft to convert the up-and-down motion of the pistons into the rotary motion required to drive the propeller shaft via the gearbox. It is connected to the pistons via connecting rods, which also use replaceable white metal bearings at their lower end where they are clamped to the crankshaft, and bronze bearings at the top where they connect to the piston via the gudgeon pin. A sump at the bottom of the engine covers the crankshaft and bearings. It is used as the reservoir for lubricating oil, which is circulated around the engine after being picked up from the sump by the oil pump, and delivered via the oil filter to all parts of the engine.

The Four-Stroke Cycle

The inlet or induction stroke begins with the piston at the top of the cylinder; the inlet valve is already open, as it opened just before the piston reached the top of its stroke. As the piston begins its descent down the cylinder it draws fresh air in through the inlet valve, which closes as the piston reaches the bottom of the first stroke.

The compression stroke begins with both the inlet and exhaust valves closed to seal the cylinder. As the piston rises it compresses the air that was drawn into the cylinder on the inlet stroke. While the air pressure rises, the air becomes hotter until maximum compression is reached at top dead centre with the air temperature reaching more than 525°C.

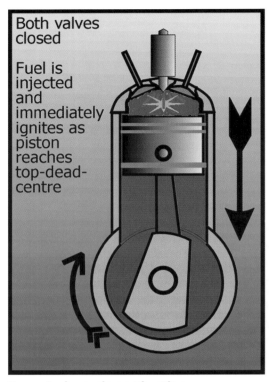

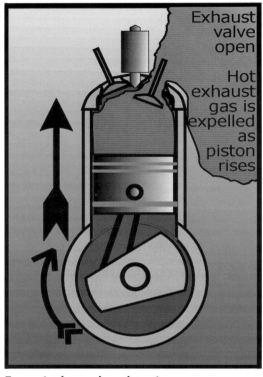

Four-stroke cycle combustion.   **Four-stroke cycle exhaust.**

The combustion or firing stroke begins just before top dead centre is reached, as the piston is still rising at the end of the compression stroke. At the appropriate moment just before top dead centre a precisely metered amount of fuel is injected at a pressure high enough to overcome the already considerable pressure within the cylinder via the injector (or atomizer) in the form of a fine spray, which is immediately ignited by the heat of the compressed air within the cylinder. As the fuel and air mixture burns, it expands rapidly, forcing the piston down the cylinder until just before bottom dead centre when the exhaust valve opens.

The exhaust stroke begins with the opening of the exhaust valve just prior to the piston beginning its ascent of the cylinder on the final stroke of the cycle. With the exhaust valve open, the piston forces the burnt gases out of the cylinder ready to accept a fresh charge of air on the next inlet stroke. The inlet valve opens just before top dead centre and while the exhaust valve is still open. This allows the fresh inlet air to be partially drawn in by the last of the exhaust gases, and also helps to ensure that the exhaust gases are completely cleared from the cylinder. The exhaust valve then closes as the fresh charge of inlet air is drawn in on the new inlet stroke.

THE TWO-STROKE DIESEL ENGINE

We will not be dealing in depth with the two-stroke diesel as it is not particularly popular in the UK with owners and operators of small craft, although there are exceptions. This section is included to indicate the differences in operation between the two-stroke and four-stroke engine should the reader ever come across a two-stroke or be contemplating buying a boat powered by one. As we have already seen, the two-stroke diesel is normally found in large, low-revving ship engines where it really excels itself, and the principle of operation is the same whether the engine is producing 10,000hp or 200hp.

As already mentioned, when the two-stroke engine was first conceived the theory existed that as it produced a firing stroke on every second stroke instead of on every fourth stroke of the four-stroke engine, it must be twice as powerful as a four-stroke of similar bore and stroke. Unfortunately, additional practical problems were found that negated a lot of the theoretical additional efficiency, and the modern two-stroke diesel is now considered to be about one and a half times more powerful than a comparable four-stroke. The biggest problem was found to be how to remove the burnt exhaust gas from the cylinder and replace it with a fresh charge of combustion air in the space of one stroke of the piston. The eventual answer was to force the fresh air into the cylinder under pressure from an air pump or supercharger.

Being mechanically driven, the air pump required a proportion of the engine's power to drive it, which further lowered the theoretical power output. However, having an excess amount of air forced into the cylinder by a supercharger ensured that exhaust gases were rapidly expelled and a plentiful charge of combustion air was available for the power stroke. This explains why the two-stroke is popular in large low-revving engines, in that the low revs allow plenty of time for the exhaust gases to be expelled from the cylinder and replaced with a charge of fresh combustion air in the space of one stroke of the piston. As engine speeds increase, the time available for the transference of exhaust gases and air becomes progressively shorter.

Unlike the four-stroke diesel engine, which is mechanically almost identical to the petrol four-stroke, the two-stroke diesel is very different to the two-stroke petrol engine used in motorcycles and outboard motors. In fact it bears more resemblance to the four-stroke diesel in that it has a heavily built block containing the cylinders, the tops of the cylinders are sealed with a cylinder head, the cylinders contain pistons connected to the crankshaft via connecting rods, and the crankshaft is located in bearing carriers at the bottom of the block, which is covered with an oil reservoir sump.

The main differences occur in the cylinder head and the cylinder itself. Instead of having inlet and exhaust passages, the two-stroke cylinder head has only an exhaust passage plus an exhaust valve controlled by a camshaft. The inlet passage is located towards the bottom of the cylinder, and enters the cylinder at the inlet port in the cylinder wall. The port opens and closes due to the movement of the piston, and has no mechanical valve gear like the exhaust valve. When the piston moves up the cylinder the piston body covers and seals the inlet port, and when it moves towards the bottom of the cylinder it uncovers the port. In practice the inlet port consists of several openings around the cylinder to allow the admission of as much air as possible in the short time that the ports are uncovered.

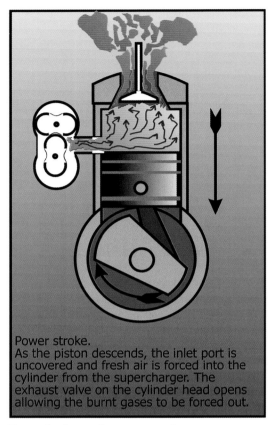

Power stroke.
As the piston descends, the inlet port is uncovered and fresh air is forced into the cylinder from the supercharger. The exhaust valve on the cylinder head opens allowing the burnt gases to be forced out.

Two-stroke cycle compression.

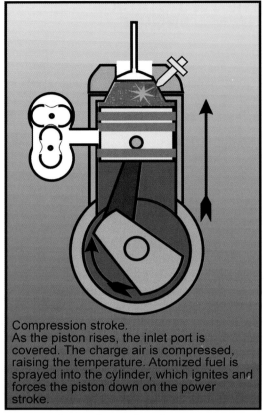

Compression stroke.
As the piston rises, the inlet port is covered. The charge air is compressed, raising the temperature. Atomized fuel is sprayed into the cylinder, which ignites and forces the piston down on the power stroke.

Two-stroke cycle combustion.

The Two-Stroke Cycle

The compression stroke begins with the piston at the bottom of the cylinder and the inlet port open as it is uncovered by the piston. The exhaust valve in the cylinder head is also open and a charge of fresh air is forced into the cylinder under pressure from the supercharger to clear the burnt exhaust gas through the exhaust valve and supply a charge of fresh air for the next combustion stroke. The exhaust valve closes and the piston begins rising up the cylinder, covering and closing the inlet port. With the cylinder now sealed, the air is compressed and the temperature increases rapidly as the piston rises.

The combustion stroke begins just before top dead centre when the precisely metered fuel is injected into the cylinder and is immediately ignited by the heat of the compressed air. As the air burns it expands and forces the piston down the cylinder. Before the piston reaches the bottom of its stroke and uncovers the inlet port, the exhaust valve opens and the still pressurized exhaust gases escape from the cylinder. As the piston reaches the bottom of the cylinder the inlet port is uncovered and pressurized air is forced into the cylinder.

CHAPTER 3

Fuel Systems

Modern diesel fuel systems are manufactured to extremely fine tolerances, but still they ask only for simple maintenance. Basically this means supplying clean, air-free fuel, and if these two criteria are met the engine will run happily and reliably. The high pressure working parts of the system, which includes the injectors and injection pump, are beyond the scope of the average boat owner to overhaul and repair: their very fine tolerances require clean, dust-free areas for dismantling if they are to retain their precision performance. Many modern injectors are no longer serviceable, and – like so much in this throw-away society – are simply discarded and replaced once worn or damaged.

By contrast, the work of removing the injectors and the injection pump for service or replacement is generally straightforward and should not present the DIY owner with any problems. There are many diesel fuel injection specialists and their prices are generally quite reasonable especially if they are mainly concerned with vehicle rather than marine engines. The fuel injection systems are identical, although prices may not be!

THE FUEL TANK

The heart of the fuel system is the fuel tank: it may be fabricated from a variety of materials including mild steel, stainless steel, aluminium or GRP. Plastic and fuel-resistant fabric materials are also used for smaller tanks.

The mild steel tank has the advantage of being cheap to construct from steel plate, and construction is also within the capabilities of the competent DIY welder using a compact arc or MIG welding plant. Lorry tanks can also be used to good advantage at low cost from commercial breakers' yards. The major disadvantage of mild steel is the possibility of corrosion occurring inside the tank due to water lying on the bottom plating. If left unattended for several years corrosion will perforate the tank bottom and cause fuel to leak into the bilges.

The simple answer is to ensure that accumulated water cannot lie at the bottom of the tank for very long: this requires that a suitable drain valve be provided in the bottom of the tank during construction. If the valve is opened for a short period every three months or so during the season any water that has collected in the tank will be removed, along with any chance of corrosion occurring.

Stainless steel and aluminium tanks are very much more expensive to buy and are less easy for the amateur to construct due to the difficulties of welding stainless steel and aluminium without more specialized equipment; even professionally built

A built-in GRP tank with plenty of baffles to prevent excess fuel movement.

Fuel feeds mounted on the inspection hatch for easy removal and cleaning.

Proper inspection hatches in the top will allow easy and regular cleaning.

tanks in these materials have been known to split when subjected to high levels of stress in rough seas. Their obvious advantage, however, is that they are generally immune to the corrosion problems that can affect mild steel tanks. GRP tanks can be built into the vessel and therefore offer maximum capacity in odd-shaped areas.

Plastic and flexible tanks do not suffer from corrosion and are generally reasonably priced. Vetus polythene tanks are popular with many builders of small boats because when installed the fuel level can be seen through the material of the tank, so there is no need for a fuel gauge. Tanks of flexible fabric must be installed carefully ensuring that no sharp projections can snag the material or rough edges chafe, as in either case this will eventually cause the tank to leak.

Refuelling
Water can enter the fuel tank when filling up with fuel. Note that many fuel storage tanks used by boatyards are never cleaned and always have a quantity of water in the fuel stocks, and this is passed on to the unsuspecting boat owner when filling his tank. Some online forums have a section where boat owners can leave reports of those places they have bought dirty fuel, and can warn others to find alternative supplies. Generally, however, yards that are always busy and sell a lot of fuel don't have the problem of water contamination, as the storage tanks are constantly being refilled with fresh, clean fuel from the refinery. This helps to avoid some of the problems of condensation that occur in storage tanks where the fuel is left for months without being renewed.

The problem of condensation also affects the on-board fuel tank and is especially prevalent during the winter lay-up when relatively large quantities of water can be produced. The answer to this particular problem is to fill the tank to the brim at the end of the season, thereby leaving no room for condensation to form. There is also a bonus in following this sensible practice in that the first tank of fuel for the new season is bought at last year's price, and as diesel fuel does not 'go stale' after a few months as petrol does, there are no problems in doing this.

Whatever precautions are taken to prevent water entering the tank it is inevitable that some will find its way in by one means or another, and this makes it essential to arrange a convenient method of draining. It is therefore not only mild steel tanks that require regular draining, as water will collect in any type of tank, and although it may not be able to corrode the bottom of stainless steel or aluminium tanks it will damage the precision fuel injection equipment if allowed to get that far. Good fuel filtration and water separation units will protect the fuel injection equipment but will themselves become quickly blocked if sediment and water are present in the tank in large quantities.

There is also a type of bacteria that will grow within diesel fuel tanks when water is present in the fuel. Once established it spreads rapidly and blocks fuel filters in a short time. It is not easy to remove, but again the simple first step to preventing it occurring is to ensure that water within the fuel tank is removed by regular draining every few months.

When draining water from a tank in this way the fuel and water which is removed can be placed in a clean receptacle and left to stand for a few hours. After this the water and any sediment will have settled to the bottom, and the clean fuel at the top can then be decanted out of the container and returned to the tank, ensuring

that fuel wastage is kept to an absolute minimum.

Draining the tank on a regular basis also removes much of the sediment and debris that collects over a period of time and which enters the tank when the filler cap is removed. Unfortunately the fuel tank is generally considered as the least important part of the fuel system, yet if more attention were paid to its cleanliness, many of the fuel-related engine problems such as blocked filters and worn injection equipment would be prevented from occurring.

It is the boat builders who must accept much of the blame for this lack of emphasis on fuel tank cleanliness, probably because cleaning the tank is not considered a very glamorous pastime; however, coming to a stop in mid-channel with dead engines is even less glamorous!

In many boats it is almost impossible to access the tanks conveniently for regular draining, and it is the exception rather than the rule to find tanks fitted with proper inspection hatches to allow the interiors to be inspected for corrosion or sediment build-up. Drain plugs are more common, although many owners are not aware of their existence.

In vessels where the tanks are difficult to access for draining, and it is suspected that water is already in the tank contaminating the fuel, there are various fuel treatments available from chandlers. Such a preparation is poured into the tank, and it breaks down the water into microscopic particles, which then bind with the fuel particles. The combined particles are small enough to pass through the fuel filters to be burned with the fuel in the engine with no loss of performance or any ill effects to either the engine or the fuel injection equipment.

These additives are preferably added to the tank prior to topping up with extra fuel, as the action of pumping in fuel causes the fuel and water already in the tank to swirl around, and in so doing ensures that the contents of the tank are well mixed.

Fuel Tank Layouts

The usual recommendation for twin engines is to have separate tanks, with each tank feeding its own engine. The reasons for this are that should one tank split, the other tank and engine will not be affected, and by using crossover valves both engines can run from either tank while the defective tank is isolated. In practice many boats have balance pipes between the tanks, a layout which negates this advantage.

The fuel feed for each engine is taken through the top of the tank, via a tube within the tank, which extends down to a point an inch or so above the bottom. This leaves room so that sediment settled on the bottom is not drawn into the fuel line. There is occasionally a small sediment sump below the feed pipe with a drain cock or plug below, and this makes regular draining a possibility.

The drawback with this conventional system is that no matter how well the tank is baffled to prevent excess fuel movement, once the fuel level drops below about 20 per cent of the tank's capacity, it is impossible to prevent air entering the feed pipe during rough weather due to the fuel slopping violently around within the tank. This means that a fuel tank with a 1,000ltr (220gal) capacity must always carry 200ltr (44gal) of fuel that cannot be used reliably.

The 'full-use' tank system that I used in my own boat has proved to have many advantages over the more conventional systems, although it is basically very simple; the fuel feed to both engines (and the diesel-fired, hot air heating system and diesel cooker) is taken from the top of a small service tank with a capacity of 10ltr (2.2gal). This is situated amidships on the engine compartment forward bulkhead below the level of the twin main tanks, which have a combined capacity of 1,350ltr (300gal), and which are situated each side of the engine compartment. The fuel feeds are incorporated into a small inspection hatch on the top of the service tank so that the interior of the tank can be inspected for

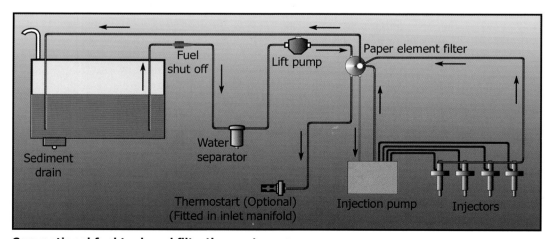

Conventional fuel tank and filtration system.

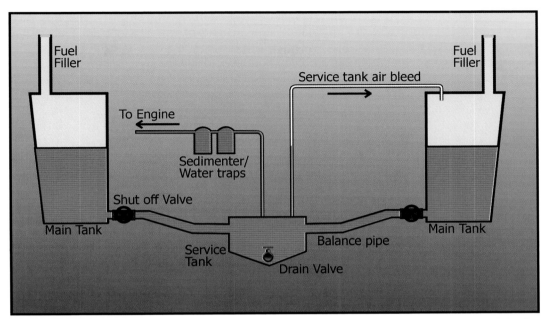

The 'full-use' tank system, allowing up to 90 per cent of fuel to be used with no risk of air entering the system.

corrosion at three-yearly intervals. Large inspection hatches are fitted to the front face of each main tank so that cleaning can be performed easily every three years.

The bottom of the service tank is shaped into a 'V' form with a slope towards the front where a 1in (2.5cm) gate valve is fitted. Fuel is gravity-fed into the service tank

A 'full-use' system service tank with drain valve.

via large bore tubes from each of the main tanks, and these tubes also act as balance pipes between the main tanks. Gate valves are fitted at the union between the balance pipe and each main tank. When running, the main tank gate valves are closed to a quarter of their normal full open setting to slow the movement of fuel between the main tanks when rolling in rough weather, and in fact are only fully opened during refuelling.

There is a fourth outlet on the top of the service tank, which is a permanent air bleed back to the main tanks designed to prevent the service tank becoming air-locked after draining or in the unlikely event of air finding its way in from either of the main tanks during rough weather.

With this system it is possible to run the tanks down to the last 100ltr (22gal) with no fear of air entering the fuel feeds due to fuel slop within the main tanks. This represents a figure of 7.5 per cent of unusable fuel against the 20 per cent of the conventional system.

Draining down is a simple matter entailing the closing of the gate valves on each of the main tanks, removing the stop plug in the end of the service tank gate valve and placing a large bucket beneath the outlet. The gate valve is then fully opened and the contents of the tank drained into the bucket. The speed of escaping fuel through the 1in gate valve ensures that most of the sediment and any water are flushed out into the bucket.

The gate valve is then closed and the stop plug replaced; this is fitted as a safeguard in case the gate valve should ever leak, and is a standard precaution with large capacity drain valves. The valves on the main tanks are opened last of all to refill the service tank, and the clean fuel in the bucket is decanted back into the main tanks after any sediment and water has settled out.

FUEL PIPING

Fuel piping from the tanks is generally run in copper as it is strong, reasonably priced and readily available from hydraulic suppliers, LPG equipment gas suppliers

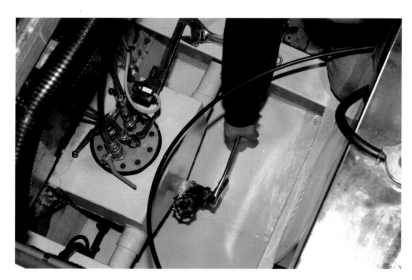

Valve for periodical draining of the service tank.

Armoured flexible fuel hose with swaged ends connecting the filter on the floor support to the engine.

Compression Joints on Fuel Piping

Compression joints are widely used on fuel systems and are extremely reliable in terms of fuel-tight integrity. They are simple to assemble and should always give perfect results. However, problems can and do occur when they are incorrectly assembled, the most common cause of problems being overtightening during assembly.

There are several types of sealing ring or olive, which are generally of either copper or brass. The most reliable in terms of effective joint sealing is the copper ring type, as copper is very much more ductile than brass and therefore adapts more easily to the compressive pressure of tightening the nut.

To prepare a joint for assembly the tube end should be cut off squarely, preferably using a proper tube cutter. These are cheap to buy and make pipe-work assembly very much quicker, especially where several joints are likely to be required. Using a tube cutter automatically ensures that the end of the tube is cut square while also placing a small chamfer on the end of the tube, making assembly easier. If a cutter is not available a junior hacksaw used carefully will do the job, although the end of the tube will need sanding down to remove all burrs before assembly.

The end of the tube to be assembled must be straight, as it is vital that the tube enters the joint at right angles. It is therefore good practice to have at least 2in (5cm) of tube before any bends. When bending tube by hand it is often difficult, if not impossible, to begin a bend close to the end of a tube without bending the end. A simple solution is to allow an extra 6in (15cm) or so of tube at the end where the fitting is to be, and after the bend is formed to cut off the excess length leaving the 2in (5cm) of straight tubing between the fitting and the start of the bend.

and plumbers' merchants, among others. As engines are nearly all flexibly mounted these days it is essential to include a flexible section in the fuel feed to connect the copper to the engine. If the copper tubing is taken directly to the engine the vibration and movement of the engine will soon cause the copper tubing to fracture.

The flexible tubing must be of the armoured type and not ordinary plastic tube. There is no place for plastic tubing anywhere in a boat's fuel system due to the lack of fire resistance and susceptibility to damage. Apart from the safety aspect, no river authorities will allow the use of plastic piping on craft using their rivers.

Two types of 'olive': copper on the left, brass on the right.

To assemble the fitting the nut is first slipped over the tube with the thread facing the fitting, followed by the copper ring. The tube end is then slipped into the fitting and pushed up against the flange inside. The copper ring is then slid up against the face of the fitting, followed by the nut, which is carefully threaded on to the fitting and hand-tightened.

Tightening the nut with a spanner while holding the joint with another will complete the job, and for small-bore fuel line sizes this should not require more than about one complete turn to effect a perfect seal.

A proper tube cutter ensures a perfect end ready for assembly.

Order of assembly for a straight compression joint.

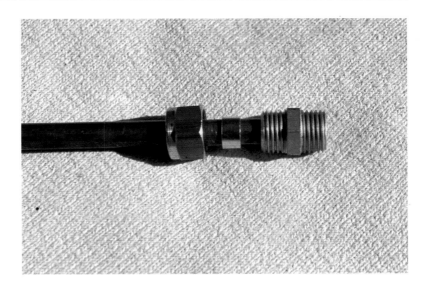

Overtightening will only distort the ring seal and crush the pipe, causing the joint to leak. It is better to under-tighten the joint as it can always be nipped up slightly later if there are any signs of leakage. When a perfect joint has been formed, it can be dismantled and reassembled many times and still form a perfect seal.

FUEL FILTRATION

The first piece of equipment after the fuel tank will be the sedimenter/water trap. It should be mounted as near to the tank as possible so there can be no chance of the pipework becoming blocked before the fuel reaches the sedimenter.

Two spanners are needed to tighten the joint.

A seriously over-tightened joint that will never seal. The pipe is crushed and the olive is almost flattened.

Sedimenters are designed with an inverted cone over which the fuel flows. Water droplets and heavy particles of sediment

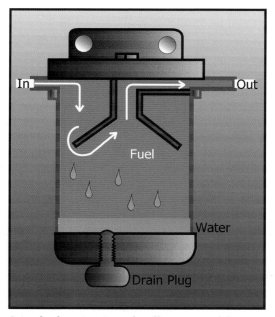

A typical water-trap/sedimenter with a drain for clearing water and debris from the reservoir at the bottom.

sink to the bottom of the unit, while the partially cleaned fuel passes out through the centre of the cone. The water and sediment can be drained off at convenient intervals, and electrical sensors are available that will alert the owner when the water and sediment has reached a predetermined level and should be drained. On many installations the sedimenter is incorporated into a twin bowl unit with a filter element in the second bowl for removing fine particles of sediment.

From the sedimenter the fuel passes to the engine fuel lift pump, which incorporates a coarse filter, and then on to the fine filter. We will look more closely at the lift pump later.

It is quite common nowadays for the fine filter to double as an agglomerator, which not only removes the very fine dirt particles remaining in the fuel, but also the tiny droplets of water. The fuel enters the unit and passes down through the element where water droplets and fine dirt particles are separated.

When the fine droplets of water are passed through a porous medium such as

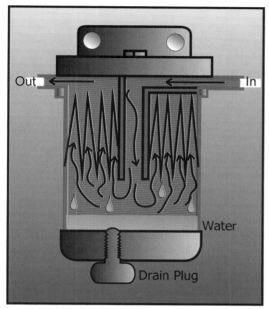

A primary filter will not trap fine water droplets as the flow is down the central tube and up through the element. Agglomerator flow is in the opposite direction, down through the filter element where fine water droplets combine and fall to the bottom of the case. Both the filter and the agglomerator have replaceable elements that require changing annually or more often if the fuel is badly contaminated.

Two pairs of heavy duty filter/ agglomerators used in place of separate sedimenters. One of each pair has a (optional) water detection sensor mounted in place of the drain plug.

the filter element, they combine into larger droplets which pass through the element and sink to the bottom of the filter body where they can be drained off in the same manner as is used with the sedimenter.

At the injection pump the fuel is precisely metered and supplied at high pressure to the injectors, where it is sprayed into the combustion chamber at the optimum moment, at the top of the compression stroke. Once the fuel has reached the injection pump and injectors it must be as clean as possible otherwise serious and costly damage will soon occur to this high

precision equipment. It is for this reason that the boat owner should pay particular attention to the cleanliness of the entire fuel system, starting with the tank.

Fuel filters are very cheap to buy and take only a few minutes to change, yet they make the difference between reliable long life and constant problems.

Changing a Fuel Filter

See the photos on pp. 35–6. As with all engine servicing, the best time to change the fuel filters is at the end of the season so that the boat is ready as soon as the first fine spring days occur. CAV equipment is common throughout the world and also very moderately priced due to its use on commercial vehicles, which also makes filter elements readily available from car accessory shops.

Sedimenters should have been drained at regular intervals throughout the summer, and can now be dismantled and thoroughly cleaned out. The majority of CAV filters, agglomerators and sedimenters used on marine engines are dismantled in the same manner, as they tend to use many common parts. There is a central bolt passing through the head of the unit to the base, and this holds the entire unit together.

A sedimenter consists of a head that is flanged for bolting to the engine or bulkhead, a sediment/water trap, and a deep base with room for water and sediment to collect and into which is fitted the drain plug. The base may be either glass or aluminium. Aluminium is the recommended material for boat use because it is less susceptible to damage, but many owners prefer to accept the slight risk of using the glass type as it is much more convenient to check for water and sediment without draining.

A filter agglomerator consists of a head, usually identical to that of the sedimenter, a disposable filter element, and a deep base, with or without a drain plug; it comes in either glass or aluminium.

A filter is virtually identical to the agglomerator using the same element; the only differences are that it utilizes a shallow base, and flow is generally in the opposite direction to that of the agglomerator, with fuel entering down the central passage of the filter and then passing up through the element. This provides slightly greater element life but offers no water separation protection, and is generally used where excessive sediment and water are not expected to be a problem.

For heavy duty cleaning, where high fuel flow is required and where longer service intervals are necessary, larger capacity long filter elements are available which will fit any of the previously mentioned units by using an extension stud to lengthen the central bolt.

Dismantling of all the above units is simply a matter of slackening the central bolt while supporting the base and filter element or sediment trap. Once the bolt is loose the lower assembly may be lowered and removed.

The filter element or sediment trap can be separated from the base, after which the rubber sealing rings are removed from the recesses in the base and head. Glass bowl types have an additional seal between the top of the glass and the filter element or sediment trap.

There is also one 'O' ring fitted below the washer under the head of the central bolt, which locates in a recess; and another round the central locating flange under the head, which separates the dirty unfiltered fuel from the clean filtered fuel. All such seals should be replaced with the filter, and are supplied for this purpose with each filter element.

There will almost certainly be some sediment in the base of all these units which may need scraping off. The base can then be rinsed in some clean fuel and dried. The sediment trap should be checked for dirt and cleaned as necessary prior to reassembly.

Reassembly is equally simple, although a little care is required to ensure that the rubber seals do not become twisted or kinked. Each seal is located into its recess in the base and head and central locating flange, and for glass bowl types the additional seal is located around the bottom of the filter element and the filter and glass assembled. A new 'O' ring is also fitted under the washer of the central bolt.

The filter element is then offered up into the head and will slip over the central flange and seal, to be followed by the base, after which the central bolt is passed through the head and located in the thread in the base. It should first be finger tightened to ensure that it is not cross-threaded, and after ensuring that all the seals are correctly located, the bolt may be tightened. The bolt should not be overtightened but 'nipped up' to bring the

1. Sedimenter (left) and filter agglomerator (right) being drained prior to dismantling. Note the date marked on the agglomerator as a reminder of when the element was last changed.

2. Undoing the central holding bolt allows the unit to be dismantled.

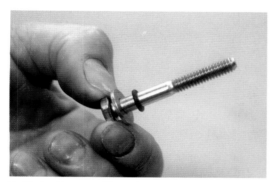

3. Note the small seal on the central holding bolt.

4. Hook out the small seal on the central flange.

5. Then do the same for the upper seal in the recess under the filter head.

6. The parts and seals of a glass bowl filter/agglomerator in order of assembly.

7. A strap or chain wrench may be needed to initially loosen spin-on fuel filters.

8. Once loose the filter can be unscrewed. Paper or rag will catch fuel drips.

9. Check that the seal is in place on top of the new element and that the old seal was removed with the old filter. Smear the new seal with clean diesel.

10. After filling the new filter with fuel, screw it on hand-tight until it feels firm.

11. Bleed the filter by slackening the screw on the filter head and operating the lift pump.

seals under pressure, which will ensure air- and fuel-tight joints.

Nowadays it is common on modern engines to use spin-on type filters for the final filter mounted on the engine. These are very easy to change as they are simply 'spun on', as the name implies. The entire filter canister is replaced and discarded, rather than a removable element being changed, as is the case with the more traditional filter.

A strap or chain wrench is usually needed to loosen the filter initially, although someone with a strong grip can often free these without assistance. Once the filter has been loosened it can be carefully unscrewed by hand. Placing paper towels underneath will catch any fuel drips as it is unscrewed. Pour the fuel remaining in the filter element into a container for disposal at the local waste oil point, or alternatively pour it into a clean container and let it stand so that any sediment can separate out, and then return it to the fuel tank.

Before disposing of the filter check that the seal on the top is in place and not stuck under the filter head on the engine; if this is the case, remove it from the filter head before fitting the new filter. Check the new filter to ensure its own seal is in place, and smear it with a drop of clean diesel.

It is then a good idea to fill the new element with clean diesel prior to refitting so as to minimize bleeding of the system. Carefully screw the filter home by hand until resistance is felt against the seal. Then finally tighten – again by hand only – until it feels firm. Finally bleed the filter by slackening the bleed screw on the filter head, and operating the lift pump until fuel flows from the bleed valve. This should not take more than a couple of pumps if the filter was filled with fuel prior to fitting. Gently tighten the bleed screw, being careful not to overdo it and strip the thread;

and finally wipe up any fuel spillage before test-running the engine.

FUEL INJECTION PUMPS

There are three types of fuel injection system in common use today, and they are hugely different. The traditional system uses an injection pump which may be of either the in-line (jerk) or rotary type. The in-line pump is more or less obsolete on modern small diesels as the rotary pump is better suited to automotive diesels, due to its lightweight and compact nature and its inherent ability to supply an equal amount of fuel to each cylinder and at the correct moment without adjustment to individual pumping elements.

The newest incarnation is the common-rail injection system, which does not have an injection pump like the older systems. Instead there is a high pressure pump that pressurizes the 'common rail' to injection pressure, and each injector is electronically controlled to open at the correct moment.

It is easy to differentiate between the two types of traditional pump, as the in-line pump has its injector pipes in a line usually on the top of the pump, while the rotary pump has its injector pipes located radially around a rotor housing at the end of the pump body.

In-Line Pumps
The in-line pump is in reality a set of separate pumps housed within a body containing a camshaft which drives each pump via its own cam. Fuel is fed into an individual pump at lift-pump pressure, and as the plunger begins to rise it seals the inlet valve in a similar manner to a two-stroke engine piston. As it continues to rise, the fuel, which is now sealed into the chamber under pressure, exerts a force on a delivery

valve which is pre-set to open at a certain pressure.

The fuel in the pump then passes into the injector pipe and forces the fuel already present within the pipe along to the injector where the needle valve opens and the fuel at high pressure is sprayed into the combustion chamber.

Meanwhile the pump plunger is still continuing to rise from the force of the cam until a helical cut-away (or helix) in the plunger clears the spill port; this immediately drops the pressure within the chamber, and the delivery valve snaps shut to cleanly end injection. Once the delivery valve in the pump closes, the pressure drops in the injector pipe and the injector needle valve closes to prevent any blowback from the combustion chamber.

The amount of fuel injected at any one time is controlled from the throttle via the fuel rack. This acts on the pump plunger to turn it within the chamber and so adjust the position of the helix and the moment at which the spill port is opened. At tick-over the helix is near to the spill port and therefore cuts off injection very quickly, but at full throttle it is much further away and allows injection to continue for much longer before opening the spill port.

Rotary Pumps

The rotary pump performs the same function except that it does it in a totally different manner: thus fuel is fed at lift-pump pressure to the pump, where it passes through the transfer pump which raises the pressure to an intermediate level. The fuel is then passed to the metering valve which regulates the amount of fuel to be passed to the rotor, and which is controlled by the throttle and governor.

The fuel then passes to the hydraulic head and enters a drilling, which at a set moment will correspond with a drilling in the rotor. Inside the rotor are two plungers that act as a pumping medium as they are moved in or out by the action of cam followers operated by internal lobes on the stationary cam ring.

As the fuel enters the rotor the plungers are pushed apart to make room for the entering fuel. As the rotor turns the drillings are closed and the fuel between the plungers is sealed into the plunger chamber.

The rotor turns further until another drilling in the hydraulic head, which is directly connected to one of the injector pipes, corresponds with the drilling in the rotor, and at the same time the plungers are forced together by the cam followers acting on the cam ring. This pushes the fuel at high pressure out of the rotor and into the injector pipe, forcing the fuel which is already present within the pipe along to the injector, where the needle valve opens and the fuel at high pressure is sprayed into the combustion chamber.

As the rotor turns further the drillings no longer correspond, and injection ends with the needle valve in the injector snapping shut to prevent blow-back from the combustion chamber in exactly the same manner as with the in-line pump.

Both types of pump can be driven via the timing gears or chain of the engine, while rotary pumps may also be driven directly from the camshaft. The timing of the injection point is dependent on correctly setting the meshing of the gears or chain. Timing marks are provided on the gears so that the engine crankshaft and camshaft and the injection pump can be aligned for correct engine operation.

Final precise injection timing of rotary pumps is set by altering the position of the pump body in relation to the pump shaft. This is achieved by turning the pump on its mounting, and locking it into position with the securing nuts. The holes in the pump flange are elongated to allow for this small amount of final adjustment.

Pump Removal
Although rotary injection pumps are mounted in different positions on different makes of engine, the method of removal and replacement is very similar for all types. The engine in the photographs is a Ford FSD, which is still a favourite with DIY marinizers. As there are so many different configurations there is no point in going into depth about one type of pump on one engine. Suffice to say that removing an injection pump is not difficult. It is vitally important that the position of the pump is marked on to its mounting before removal to ensure that it is easy to refit and that the injection timing is not altered. Once again, this is an area where every make of engine is different, so if the timing needs adjusting for any reason it will be necessary to refer to the engine workshop manual for details.

This particular engine in the photograph has the injection pump mounted behind the timing cover and is driven via the timing belt in sequence with the crankshaft and camshaft. The pump shaft is keyed, which ensures that it can only be fitted in one position in relation to the timing belt. The final pump timing on this engine is performed by moving the cam-belt gear on the pump mounting flange. It is sensible to mark the position of the timing belt on all three gears – injection pump, camshaft, crankshaft – before removing the timing belt to enable the pump to be removed.

The pump is secured with three mounting bolts behind the timing gear, which makes it impossible to remove the pump without disturbing the belt.

On many other engines the pump mounting flange is a scribed line that should correspond with another scribed line on the engine flange. It does not always correspond exactly, as the pump may at some previous time have been overhauled and reset slightly differently internally, which has meant setting it up on the engine in a slightly different position. If this is found to be the case, then the flange should be re-marked before moving the pump so that both lines correspond, thereby ensuring

The timing belt has to be removed before this pump can be unbolted.

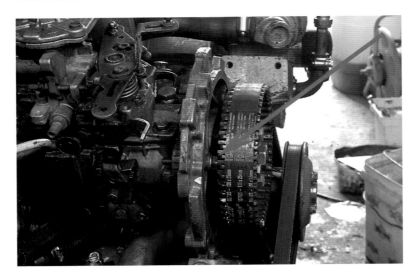

Once the belt and timing gear is off there are three bolts to undo to free the pump.

that the pump is refitted in the same position. Removal is then a straightforward operation.

Before beginning removal of any type of pump it is worthwhile cleaning the area around the pump and the pump itself to prevent dirt entering once the pipework is disconnected. Both ends of the injector pipes should be disconnected so they can be removed completely. Injector pipes must never be bent out of the way as they are liable to snap or become kinked and weakened.

In the same manner, if the inlet and return pipes to the pump are in the way they should also be removed completely to avoid damage. Once the pipework is out of the way the pump securing nuts may be removed complete with washers and the pump carefully slid away from the engine, disengaging the splines in the drive. It can then be emptied of fuel by inverting it, and if plastic blanking plugs are available they should be fitted into or over all the pipe unions, and the pump immediately placed in a clean plastic bag to keep dirt and damp out. Plastic blanking plugs are available from diesel engineers, who will usually supply a handful if the pump is being taken in to them for service.

Once the fuel pump is removed, the gasket between the pump and engine-mounting flanges should be removed and discarded.

When installing the pump after service a fresh gasket should be fitted dry to the engine flange. If sealant is used it will make it impossible to alter the position of the pump for final lining up of the scribed lines on the flanges without tearing the gasket.

The key or master spline on the pump shaft should be positioned so that it corresponds with the position of the keyway or master spline in the engine drive. This can usually be seen by shining a torch into the drive; alternatively, if the engine is positioned where it is impossible to see into the drive, the position of the master spline can often be found by feeling inside the drive with a fingertip.

With both splines roughly aligned, the pump may be offered up into position and gently turned to locate the master splines. It must never be forced, as damage may occur, and in any case once the master splines are aligned the pump will slide smoothly into place with ease. The timing marks can now be accurately aligned and the securing nuts tightened.

In-line pumps are usually solidly mounted on the engine with either a flange mounting similar to the rotary pump or a steel strap. An external coupling is used to transmit the drive from the engine timing gears to the pump, and this removes any slight misalignment between engine and pump.

As with the rotary pump, it is worth cleaning down the area around the pump before disconnecting the pipework to prevent dirt entering the pump.

With the pump mounting nuts or strap unfastened, the pump can usually be lifted away from the engine by sliding the coupling apart. There is no gasket to remove as the drive coupling shaft has its own oil seal, which is not disturbed during pump removal. The pipe unions should be sealed with plastic blanking caps and the pump placed in a clean plastic bag.

Refitting the in-line pump is slightly more complex than the rotary as there is no master spline to ensure that the pump timing is automatically set. The engine must be turned until number one piston is near the top of its compression stroke, which can be ascertained with the injector removed by placing a long rod into the injector orifice to check that the piston is rising and that the inlet and exhaust valve are closed. Ensure that the rod is too long to drop inside the cylinder, and that it does not jam between the piston and cylinder head.

When both valves are closed their rockers will have a slight free movement up and down indicating that the valve springs are not under compression and that the valves are therefore closed. If the piston is rising on the exhaust stroke, the exhaust valve will be closing, indicating that the engine must be turned through another complete revolution before the compression stroke is reached.

The engine manual will indicate where the injection timing marks are located on the engine, which may be on the flywheel at the rear of the engine or the crankshaft pulley at the front. A fixed pointer will also be fitted, which must be aligned with the timing mark by further turning of the engine. If the mark is passed the engine should be turned back well past the mark before turning it forwards again, as this will remove any backlash in the gears or chain which could affect accuracy when aligning the pump coupling.

With this position set, the pump coupling must be turned to align the timing mark on the case with the mark on the pump shaft. The pump can now be refitted and the coupling connected.

With both types of pump, care should be exercised when reconnecting the pipework to ensure that each pipe is run to its correct position. Injector pipes are preformed, and each will only fit between the pump and the correct injector. If a pipe seems to require a lot of bending it is almost certainly fitted to the wrong injector and pump union.

COMMON-RAIL INJECTION

The common-rail system has been around since about 1997 and was the biggest single breakthrough in modern diesel technology. To provide the very best performance and economy from a diesel engine, every part of the injection and combustion process is computer monitored and controlled. This technology has allowed diesel engines to achieve the smooth, quiet running of their petrol counterparts, with even better fuel economy. Despite this, the basic engine is still the same unit and needs the same maintenance as any other diesel.

The difference is all in the injection system, which works in a completely different way to what may be called standard injection. Instead of having a fuel injection pump that pressurizes the fuel and feeds it to the appropriate injector at a given moment as the piston approaches top dead centre, there is a fuel pressurization pump that constantly maintains full injection pressure within the 'common rail' at all times, even at low engine speeds. When starting the engine there is always a lag of one or two turns of the engine before it fires, as the pressurization pump raises the common-rail pressure. Once full pressure is achieved

the sensor allows the injectors to begin operating and the engine starts immediately, with no smoky emissions from the exhaust.

The injectors are more or less identical to standard system types except they are operated electronically to provide optimum power and minimum emissions, and the amount of fuel being injected is decided by the sensors in various parts of the engine. The throttle position is the most obvious sensor, but also the air mass sensor that detects the amount of air available for the combustion process at any given time. This ensures that too much fuel cannot be injected despite the position of the throttle, as this would cause increased emissions.

Another huge plus with electronic control of the injectors is that 'pilot injection' is now possible, which allows a very small measure of fuel to be injected into

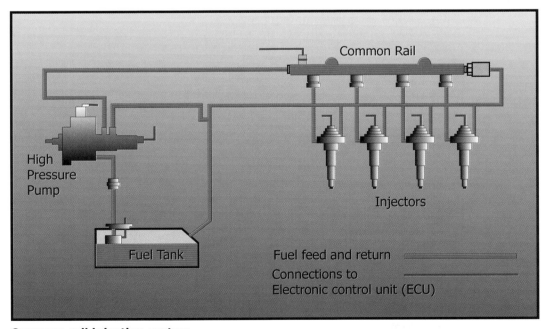

Common-rail injection system.

the cylinder just prior to the main injection point. This ensures that the fuel entering on the main injection burns more thoroughly as the combustion process has already started, but it also smoothes the pressure build-up within the cylinder on the power stroke and dramatically reduces diesel knock, which gives the engine its more petrol-like sound.

FUEL INJECTORS

The operation of an injector is directly controlled by the action of the injection pump forcing fuel under pressure along the injector pipe to the injector; apart from this it has no mechanical drive of any sort.

As with the injection pump, an injector should only be dismantled in clean room conditions where the appropriate equipment for testing, cleaning, repair and resetting are available. Without the correct pressure-testing equipment to reset the pressure at which injection takes place the injector will not function correctly and may dribble, causing violent knocking within the engine due to excess fuel entering the combustion chamber and causing excessive combustion pressure to build up.

Injectors on many new engines are now throwaway items, but the need for cleanliness is still good practice as it prevents dirt entering the pipe once the injector is removed.

Removing Older Injectors
See the photos on pp. 43–44. The leak-off pipes connect all the injectors, with the leak-off connection on top of the fuel filter, and then lead back to the top of the fuel tank where excess fuel and small quantities of air (if present) are returned. 'Banjo' unions are often used, so called because of their vague similarity to a banjo shape! The central bolt is slackened and carefully removed. The soft aluminium or copper washers used to form a seal between the holding-down bolt and the banjo are again carefully retained during disassembly. There are two to each union.

The pre-formed steel injector pipes must be distorted as little as possible when disconnecting from the injector. On larger engines where the pipework is generally quite long it is permissible to gently ease the pipes away from the injectors as the nuts are unscrewed, rather than removing them completely. Many injectors are held in the cylinder head with two studs and nuts. The nuts must be removed by slackening them equally a little at a time

1. Disconnect the leak-off pipe.

2. Take care to save the sealing washers.

3. Undo the injector pipe nut.

4. Evenly slacken the injector holding bolts.

5. Use penetrating oil to help free a stuck injector.

6. Lightly hammer round the injector to start it moving.

7. Once free, lift the injector out.

8. Hook out the sealing washer if it didn't come out with the injector.

to avoid distortion of the injector. It is good practice to cover the end of the injector pipe once it is disconnected to avoid the ingress of dirt.

An injector that has been in position for several years will probably be reluctant to move from its bore, as carbon deposits will have built up around the tip. A generous application of penetrating oil around the injector body and into the bore helps to break up the corrosion seal. Leave it to soak for a few minutes (or a few hours if really stubborn) before attempting to move the injector. A light tap with a soft-faced hammer (or lightly hammering against a block of wood) around the body is usually sufficient to free it off ready for removal. If it is particularly obstinate a bar may be needed under the securing flange to lever it upwards while gently tapping around the body. Ensure that the bar cannot distort the securing studs while levering, and do not exert excessive force in any one position. Patience and light tapping will eventually do the trick.

Once the injector begins to move it can be lifted out of its bore. With the injector removed, check that the copper sealing washer is still attached to the end of the injector body. If it is not, it will be found at the bottom of the injector bore and should be hooked out with the end of a screwdriver or similar tool. *Be particularly careful to ensure that the tool cannot drop inside the cylinder, otherwise what should have been a simple job will become a major cylinder head removal task!*

When refitting an injector the copper sealing washer must be renewed: new ones are generally supplied when injectors are overhauled. If for any reason new washers are not available, the old ones may be annealed to renew their sealing properties by heating to a cherry red with a blowlamp (or over the cooker) and plunging into cold water.

The new washer is fitted over the end of the injector body prior to the injector being replaced into its bore in the head. The securing nuts should then be run down the studs an equal amount until they are finger tight, finally tightening both down equally with a socket or spanner to ensure a gas-tight seal.

Removing Modern Injectors
See the photos on pp. 45–46. Injector removal is a simple task for the DIY owner. The first task is to disconnect the leak-off pipes on the top of the injectors. These may be either a push-fit or proper joints that need slackening and disconnecting. Once

1. Once the leak-off pipe is disconnected the injection pipe nut can be slackened.

2. Once slack, it is undone completely.

3. The other end is then removed from the injection pump.

4. The piping can then be removed and laid to one side.

5. The securing nut (or nuts) on the injector can now be slackened . . .

6. . . . and removed.

7. If you are lucky the injector will simply pull out of the head.

8. Once it is out, the body can be cleaned of carbon if the injector is to be refitted.

these are off, the injection pipe nut must be slackened and then unscrewed completely.

Injectors are secured into the cylinder head with one or two studs and nuts, which must be removed by slackening equally.

The injector may be reluctant to move from its bore as carbon deposits may have built up around the tip, however a light tap with a soft-faced hammer around the body will usually free it off sufficiently for removal. If it is particularly obstinate a bar may be needed under the securing flange to lever it upwards while gently tapping around the body. Ensure that the bar cannot distort the securing studs while levering. Leaving it soaking in penetrating fluid for several days may eventually help to release it, but in the worst case with modern lightweight injectors there may be no alternative than to hammer it out, which will usually mean a replacement is needed.

Volvo Injectors

Some Volvo injectors (certain engine models only) are fitted into sealing sleeves that require a special tool for injector removal. If the tool is not used and the sleeve be-comes disturbed during extraction the cylinder head will have to be removed in order to fit a new sleeve.

In all cases if once the engine is started there is evidence of blow-by from an injector, the two most likely causes are either that the sealing washer has been inadvertently omitted or the securing nuts have been tightened unevenly. The solution to both problems is obvious!

FUEL LIFT PUMPS

Diaphragm-type lift pumps are the most common in small to mid-range diesels and are a fairly simple piece of equipment. They consist of a two-part body that contains a diaphragm secured around its periphery and forming a seal between the upper and lower halves of the body. A coarse gauze filter is sometimes located in the upper half of the pump, along with the simple spring-loaded inlet and outlet valves above the diaphragm. (certain engine models only)

The centre of the diaphragm is sandwiched between two metal discs attached

A Volvo injector removed using the special tool.

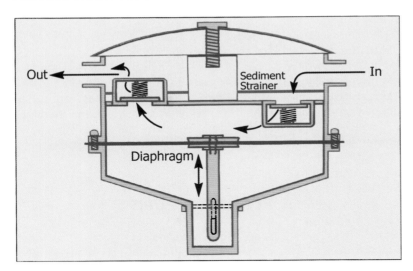

Diagram of a common lift fuel pump.

to a pull rod below the diaphragm. A return spring acts on the lower metal disc of the diaphragm to maintain its centralized position. The pull rod is attached to a two-part operating arm which is pivoted within the pump body and driven from the engine camshaft.

When the operating arm is moved by the camshaft it exerts a downward pressure on the diaphragm against spring pressure via the pull rod, which causes fuel to be drawn into the chamber through the inlet valve. As the operating arm returns, spring pressure causes the diaphragm to return to the

The coarse screen in the top of the lift pump.

central position which forces the fuel from the chamber through the outlet valve.

When fuel pressure on the outlet side rises to a point where it is greater than the return spring pressure, it simply holds the diaphragm down so that no more fuel is pumped until the pressure begins to drop as fuel is used. As soon as there is a small drop in pressure the diaphragm is allowed to move up and pump additional fuel. While the diaphragm is stationary the operating arm continues to move under the influence of the camshaft, but the two-part design means that only the part in contact with the camshaft moves, while the part attached to the pull rod remains stationary with the diaphragm.

Should the diaphragm be damaged the pump will cease to operate, and in an emergency a gravity feed may be set up to bypass the pump to keep the engine running.

There is little maintenance required for the diaphragm-type pump, except to clean the coarse gauze filter once a season during annual maintenance, and to remove any residue found in the pump body.

Plunger-type lift pumps operate in a similar manner but are generally located on in-line injection pumps and are driven from the pump camshaft. They would normally be serviced with the injection pump.

BLEEDING THE FUEL SYSTEM

Once the fuel system has been disturbed and pipe unions opened it will be necessary to bleed the system to purge it of air. Most modern engines are now self-bleeding and only need the engine to be turned on the starter to clear the filters and injector pump of air. However, the injectors still need bleeding to finalize the job.

On older engines that require manual bleeding of the entire system this is a simple job – assuming that all pipe joints and filter seals have been correctly refitted and are effecting a proper seal! If after much priming it is found that air is still in the system, it is a fair assumption that there is an air leak somewhere on the suction

Small bleed valves on a typical older fuel injection pump.

(fuel tank) side of the lift pump. Any leaks on the pressure (injection pump) side of the lift pump will not cause air to enter the system, they will simply allow fuel to escape and can be checked visually.

With the fuel system completely empty after a thorough overhaul including removal of the injection pump for maintenance, replacement of fuel filter elements and cleaning of the lift pump, it will take a few minutes of manually pumping the lift pump to fill the system with fuel.

The first task is to slacken all the bleed vents throughout the system. There is usually one on top of the filter, but if not, the fuel outlet union to the injection pump may be slackened off for this purpose. There are normally two on rotary injection pumps: one on the pump body and one at the top of the governor housing. These will need only one turn to slacken them sufficiently. If they are undone completely there is a danger of them being dropped into the bilge and lost.

With all vents open, the lift pump may be operated. If there is no resistance felt when pumping manually, the operating arm may be resting on the top of its cam, preventing the pump from operating. Turning the engine over manually half a turn will move the camshaft and drop the operating arm, allowing manual pumping.

The manual lever should be operated until fuel with no signs of any bubbles is being emitted, first from the filter, at which point the bleed screw or outlet union can be tightened, followed by the injection pump bleed unions. If a tray can be set up to catch the lost fuel it will help to keep the bilge clean.

Once the system is free of air and all the unions are tight, two of the injector pipe unions can be slackened at the injectors to bleed air from the high pressure side of the pump and the injector pipes them-

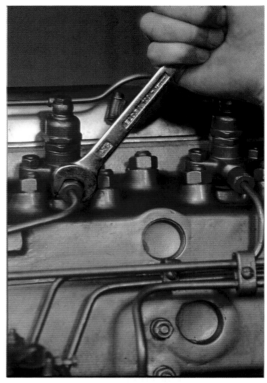

Injector pipe unions need to be slackened to complete the bleeding process.

selves. Although slackening them a couple of turns is sufficient to allow air to escape, it is often worth disconnecting one completely so that the amount of fuel being expelled from the pipe union can be seen.

The engine throttle should be set to maximum and the stop control checked to ensure that it is in the run position, and the engine may then be cranked over on the starter while watching the amount of fuel being expelled from the pipe. If no fuel is expelled, or if there is only the occasional dribble, this will indicate that the injection pump requires further bleeding.

If a good charge of fuel is expelled while cranking the engine, and smoke is seen to be emitted from the exhaust, this will indicate that the system is free from air and that injection is taking place. Many direct injection engines will actually start and run at this point, even with two injector pipe unions disconnected. If this happens the engine should be stopped and the unions reconnected. Indirect injection engines will need the normal cold start procedure at this point to get them running.

COLD STARTING AIDS

There are four main types of cold starting aid in general use at the moment: heater plugs, the Thermostart, excess fuel and ether.

Heater Plugs
The most popular type of cold starting aid is the heater plug. A separate plug is screwed into each combustion chamber, and consists of an electrically operated heating coil inside the chamber which warms the air to assist with initial combustion. To operate, either a button is depressed for thirty seconds or, in the latest engines, an automatic

timer does the job, after which the chamber is warm enough for the engine to fire as soon as it is turned on the starter. The plugs are not serviceable, however, and they either work or they don't!

To test them on a cold engine, simply press the button or operate the timer and after thirty seconds feel each plug to ensure that it is warm. Any that are defective will remain cold. Replacing a defective is simply a matter of unscrewing the old plug and replacing it with a new one, although care must be taken to ensure that the old plug does not shear off as it is being removed, otherwise the cylinder head will need to be removed to get at the broken piece.

'Thermostart'
The 'Thermostart' is the most popular type of cold starting aid for older engines, and again consists of an electrically operated heating coil; however, in this case only one unit is fitted, and this is situated in the inlet manifold. As the coil heats up it opens a ball valve, which allows diesel fuel on to the heating coil: this immediately bursts into flame when the engine is turned on

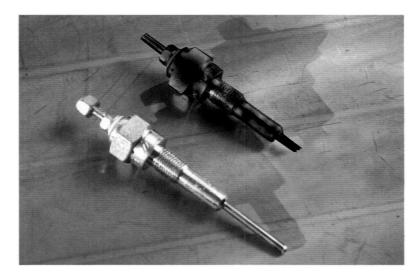

Typical heater plugs, one new, the other burned out and broken.

A CAV Thermostart. The heating element that opens the ball valve can be clearly seen inside.

the starter. The flame is drawn into the cylinders and raises the temperature to ease starting. As direct injection engines are easy to start in most conditions, the 'Thermostart' is usually only needed in the coldest of winter weather.

Once again they are non serviceable, and should be replaced if defective. To test a 'Thermostart' is simply a matter of operating the switch or button and observing the unit for smoke, which should appear after a few seconds. If left on it will eventually burst into flame, showing that it is working correctly. If it remains cold it is either defective, or there is a fault in the wiring, or possibly a blown fuse.

Early examples of this type of cold start device were fed from a reservoir that had to be topped up manually, while later models used a small reservoir fed from the fuel return to the tank. However, the latest engines use a direct feed from the fuel filter, which removes the need for reservoirs. The 'Thermostarts' themselves are identical, and it is therefore perfectly feasible to update early systems to direct feed and remove the additional pipework and reservoirs, thereby simplifying the system.

A Thermostart can usefully be used in place of defective, corroded-in heater plugs where the cylinder head cannot be conveniently removed to replace them. It is installed in the air cleaner housing and connected to the spare outlet on the engine fuel filter. I did this on a BMC 1.5 some years ago and it worked perfectly for several years until I took the head off and renewed the proper heater plugs.

Excess Fuel
The excess fuel device consists of a manually operated button on the side of the injection pump, which causes the fuel rack to open past its maximum fuel position to allow a large volume of fuel to enter the cylinder on the first turn of the engine. Once the engine has fired it automatically resets itself to the normal run position.

Ether
The ether system uses a highly flammable liquid which is sprayed into the cylinder while the engine is being turned on the starter. It is basically the same as the 'Easy Start' aerosols that many owners of worn-out engines resort to for starting, except that the system is installed within the engine compartment and can be remotely operated. It is generally only used on large, specialized engines and is unlikely to be found on small to medium-sized marine engines.

CHAPTER 4

Lubrication

Just as the fuel system needs clean fuel to keep the engine running smoothly, the lubrication system requires regular changes of the oil and filter to ensure that engine wear is kept to a minimum and that all the internal components remain at their proper temperature while running. Oil is very much more than a simple lubricant when used in a marine diesel engine as it not only provides effective lubrication when the engine is running, but also acts as a cleaning agent, carrying away harmful oxide deposits. Two other very important functions of the lubricating oil are its role as a cooling medium, carrying away heat from high temperature areas while also providing a degree of protection from corrosion when the engine is left standing idle during the lay-up period.

Modern oils include many additives that offer greater 'slipperiness' for improved lubrication and lower friction between moving parts, plus corrosion inhibitors to coat the internal surfaces when the engine is idle. It is true to say that the more expensive the oil, the higher is the additive content and therefore the protection offered to the engine.

The most sophisticated oils are those designed for turbocharged engines (which nowadays include all but the smallest and lowest-powered units). These engines work under greater stresses than naturally aspirated (non-turbocharged) units, so the oil must also provide effective lubrication for the turbocharger, which may be running at anything up to 100,000rpm.

Although it is absolutely essential to use the correct grade of oil on turbocharged engines, it will equally benefit the naturally aspirated engine to use these top quality grades. The choice of whether or not to use a detergent oil depends on the type of engine, where it is operated, and under what conditions. Detergent oils clean the engine and carry the products of combustion in suspension, thereby preventing the build-up of oxidization on the internal surfaces. This is why a detergent oil will very quickly become blackened after an oil change, as it rapidly collects the residue of the old oil remaining in the engine.

Modern oils designed for petrol engines are generally also suitable for non-turbo-diesel engines, and a quick check on the specification label on the can will confirm this. However, the use of non-detergent oils causes a gradual build-up of oxide within the engine. If a change is made to detergent oil after using non-detergent for a long period of time it will usually be necessary to flush the engine through at least once to remove the excess combustion products, which may be carried around in lumps within the engine after the initial change.

The filter may also require changing several times in a short period after the changeover, but once the detergent oil has done its work the oil change periods can revert to normal practice.

Synthetic and semi-synthetic oils are now readily available, and these offer even greater protection to the engine. However, owners of older engines should take care if considering these modern oils, because they have a thin film thickness designed for the close tolerance engineering of modern engines, and this may be unsuitable for earlier engines, which need a heavier film thickness to maintain the proper lubrication properties for the engine. Generally speaking it is sensible to use the type and grade of oil that was available when the engine was new, as the engine was designed and built with this type of oil in mind.

THE LUBRICATION SYSTEM

The lubrication system is a fairly straightforward arrangement, and apart from a general understanding of the way the oil is circulated and the work it performs on the way, there is not a great deal to attend to in the matter of maintenance.

The oil is stored within a sump at the bottom of the engine below the crankcase or block. It is filled via the oil filler cap on top of the rocker or cam cover on the top of the engine. In some cases an

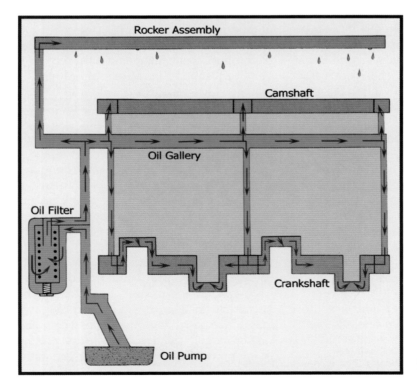

A typical lubricating oil system.

additional filler is provided on the side of the sump for ease of topping up when the engine is tightly installed below the deck-head.

From the sump the oil is drawn up via a coarse strainer by the oil pump, which is generally of the gear type driven from the timing gears at the front of the engine. The oil pressure relief valve may be incorporated into the pump, and if so is beyond the attention of day-to-day maintenance;

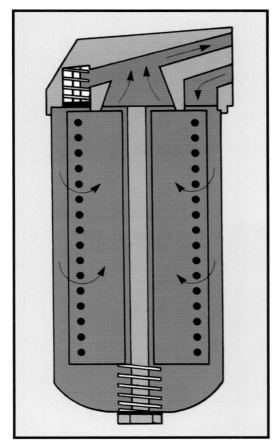

Cross-section of an oil filter with a pressure relief valve to allow oil to bypass the filter if it becomes totally blocked.

alternatively it may be set into the oil filter assembly where it can be dismantled for cleaning if the oil's pressure suddenly rises or falls. Generally speaking these only stick after months or years of the engine remaining idle, and in normal use will never need attention.

From the pump the oil, now under pressure, passes to the oil filter – often via an oil cooler – where it is cleaned of impurities and ready to be circulated around the engine. It then passes into the oil gallery where it is fed to the crankshaft main bearings. A channel in the face of the bearings takes the oil right round the journal and the bearing surfaces.

From the main bearings the oil is fed into drillings through the centre of the crankshaft to each individual big end bearing. Depending on the engine design, the small end bearings, which are located at the top of the connecting rods, are either fed with a supply of oil via a drilling through the connecting rod, or via a spray system where a drilling through the big end lines up with the drilling in the crankshaft once every revolution, and sprays oil under pressure up into the base of the piston where it flows on to the small end bearing. Many high-powered engines, especially turbocharged models, have additional piston cooling arrangements whereby oil is sprayed up under the piston crown where it may enter passages within the crown to circulate for maximum cooling effect before draining out and back into the sump.

Oil is also fed directly either from the gallery or the main bearings into the camshaft bearings via drillings in the block, finally arriving at the head and the valve rocker assembly, where it drains back via the timing gears into the sump to be picked up again, cleaned within the filter, and recirculated.

Turbocharged engines generally utilize oil directly from the clean side of the filter via a pipe direct to the turbocharger bearings, which are lubricated and cooled before the oil drains back into the sump.

MAINTENANCE

The two most important items of regular maintenance for the DIY owner are the regular changing of the engine oil and filter. If these slightly unpleasant tasks are performed at the intervals laid down in the manufacturer's instructions, and the correct grade of engine oil is used, the life of the engine will be greatly enhanced compared with one that is neglected. The old saying that 'pleasure boat engines corrode away before they can wear out' can also be more or less discounted with the use of high quality oils incorporating corrosion inhibitors.

Changing the oil is a messy business at the best of times, and to avoid spread-ing spilt oil everywhere it is worthwhile to spread copious amounts of old newspaper all round the working area and under the engine itself. Before beginning the job of draining the oil the engine should be run to thoroughly warm the oil so that it will flow freely when draining.

If the engine is mounted high enough to allow the use of a drain tray beneath the sump the oil may be drained in the conventional manner via the sump drain plug. However, before even beginning the job ensure that there is sufficient room to get the full drain tray out from under the engine without having to tilt it! If the tray can only be removed by tilting it, a large air-tight food container will do the trick. Once it is full of oil, snap on the lid and the oil is sealed in, allowing the container to be tilted to any angle without fear of oil spillage.

The majority of installations, however, will have insufficient clearance for a drain tray, and the oil will therefore have to be pumped out. Many engine manufacturers

Using a snap-lid food container to drain oil from the sump.

incorporate a sump pump in their standard engine specification, which means that all that is required is to operate the pump by hand to remove the oil, which can be pumped straight into an old oil can. For engines without a built-in pump there are several hand and electrically operated pumps available, which are supplied with special small bore tubes to fit down the dipstick hole. I use an electric model that works very well, and drains an 18ltr (4gal) sump in about two minutes.

Once the oil is drained the sump plug should be replaced and tightened immediately, and the engine can then be topped up with the new oil. The engine manufacturer's specification will usually include the oil capacity for a simple oil change, as well as the additional capacity when the filter is changed. As the filter should always be changed on a marine engine when the oil is changed, the latter capacity is the one to take note of.

Whether the oil is replaced before or after the filter is changed is really immaterial, as the new oil will be unable to enter the filter until the engine is run, but many owners prefer to drain the old oil and change the filter before topping up with fresh oil.

Changing Spin-On Oil Filters
See the photos on p. 58. Changing the filter on a modern engine is simplicity itself, as 'spin-on' filters are now the standard fitting. These filters are easily distinguishable from paper element filters in that they are simply a plain canister, usually with the maker's name displayed on the side. The paper element-type filter has a central securing bolt through the bottom of the filter case.

To remove a 'spin-on' filter, all that is required is to unscrew it and discard the entire assembly. As they tend to be a rather tight fit, after a year on the engine a proper filter remover will be needed. These

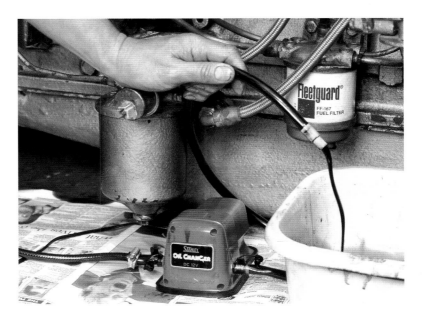

A low-cost, 12-volt oil drain pump.

1. Use a filter wrench to remove the old filter.

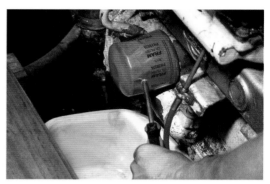

2. In an emergency, stab the old filter with a screwdriver to provide leverage.

3. Check that the seal is in place on top of the old filter.

4. Smear a little engine oil on to the seal of the new filter.

5. Hand-tighten the new filter; it does not need tightening with the wrench.

are normally a belt and lever arrangement, where the belt is wrapped around the canister and as pressure on the lever is applied, the belt tightens on the canister allowing plenty of leverage for unscrewing even the most stubborn filters. The nasty emergency alternative is to 'stab' the canister body with a large screwdriver, and use this to provide the necessary leverage for unscrewing.

Once the old filter is removed, check that the seal on the top is in place (the same as with spin-on fuel filters). If it is missing it has either fallen off during removal, or is stuck to the mounting face on the block and must be removed. If the new filter is screwed on and the new seal sits on top of the old one it is likely that the pressure of the oil will blow oil out between the seals.

Before fitting the new filter, smear a drop of clean engine oil on to the seal at the top of the canister. The canister can then be screwed home as tightly as possible by hand pressure alone.

Changing Paper Element Filters

To change the older paper element filter requires a little more care than with the 'spin-on' type, as there is a seal at the top which must be replaced when the filter is changed.

The bolt at the bottom of the filter case is slackened with an appropriate-sized spanner or socket until the case containing the filter element can be removed. For conventionally mounted filter bodies with the case hanging down, care will be needed to avoid dropping oil everywhere during this operation as the case and element holds around a pint (half a litre) of oil. (For filters mounted upside down the oil will have drained down and the problem will not arise.)

Once the case is removed the filter element can be extracted and discarded, being particularly careful to save any mounting washer that may have become stuck to the bottom of the element. This mounting washer sits on a spring in the bottom of the case and ensures that the filter element is securely held against the inlet and outlet oil ports within the filter head when assembled.

Under the head of the filter assembly is a recessed groove around the edge: this locates the sealing washer, which forms a seal with the lip of the case when reassembled. This must be hooked out using a suitable implement such as a penknife blade

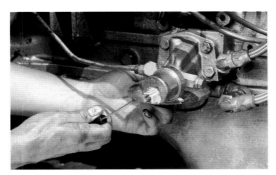

Make sure the old seal is pulled out from under the mounting head.

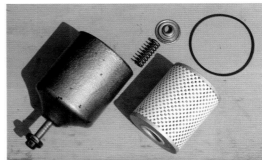

The components and seals of an older paper element filter assembly.

or a small screwdriver. In many cases a new filter element will be provided with two or more new sealing washers to accommodate the filter arrangements of several different makes or models of engine, and it is therefore important to select the correct seal before reassembly by comparing the new seals with the old one.

The correct seal may then be fitted into the recess in the filter head, ensuring that it is sitting squarely within the recess and is not kinked or twisted. If it tends to drop out, a small dab of grease will keep it in position. The filter case should be cleaned out to remove all the old oil residue and any swarf that has congregated at the bottom; wiping this out with a clean paper towel is the most effective method. The new filter element can then be fitted on to the spring and washer within the base of the case, and the entire assembly offered up under the filter head. The case may need to be held up against spring pressure until the locating bolt is screwed home. Before finally tightening the bolt, ensure that the lip of the case is evenly located within the recess around the head so that it compresses the seal to ensure an oil-tight joint. The bolt can then be finally 'snugged up', avoiding overtightening.

Oil Leaks

The final maintenance item within the field of the lubrication system concerns oil leaks. Minor oil leaks are little more than an annoyance and won't affect the performance or life of the engine, but major leaks if undetected could cause the engine to seize, resulting in major damage. To prevent an oil leak of this type, an audible warning of loss of oil pressure is worth arranging. Further details of a DIY audible alarm is shown in the chapter on electrical systems. These are particularly useful nowadays as many boats extensively use autopilots,

which means the instruments are not being monitored by the helmsman. An audible warning will quickly draw everyone's attention to the fact that a problem has arisen.

Happily the majority of oil leaks are of the minor type and merely spoil an otherwise clean engine compartment if left unattended, so attention as soon as possible after they are discovered is recommended. Many leaks can be simply cured by tightening the securing bolts or nuts on whatever panel or casing the oil is escaping from. However, care is required not to overtighten these, as this will probably damage the gasket beyond repair by either crushing or splitting it. If the leak persists the only course of action is to replace the gasket with a new one.

When removing an old gasket it is essential to clean off every trace from the mating surfaces so that the new gasket has a perfectly smooth surface on which to form the seal. It is worth consulting the workshop manual before fitting a new gasket, as some types of gasket are designed to expand when in contact with oil and are therefore best assembled without any gasket sealant being applied.

The majority of cork gaskets will benefit from the application of a smear of gasket sealant of whichever type the owner prefers, although one of the most popular makes for general use is 'Hylomar', readily available from car accessory shops. With both surfaces clean, the gasket sealant is applied in a thin layer on to one face, after which the gasket is fitted into place. The other face is then coated with sealant and the panel or casing fitted into position. The securing nuts or bolts can be lightly tightened until all surfaces are in contact, then after pausing for a few minutes to allow the solvents within the sealant to evaporate, the job can be finally tightened, again ensuring that the join is not overtightened.

The rocker or cam-cover gasket is often one that gives problems, and is particularly annoying as any leaks from here will run right down the engine causing the maximum amount of mess. These gaskets are generally fitted dry to allow easy removal of the rocker/cam cover for periodical valve clearance adjustment. However, these gaskets have an annoying tendency to slip inside the cover as the bolts are being tightened, so to prevent this happening I make a point of smearing one side of the gasket with sealant and then positioning it on to the face of the cover and leaving it until it has stuck in place. It is then possible with care to position the cover on to the engine and tighten the bolts without the gasket moving.

Probably the worst possible leak of a minor nature is that from the crankshaft rear oil seal. On old engines this was in the form of a graphite-impregnated rope, quite similar in appearance to stern gland packing except that it is round in section while packing is square. To replace this type of seal requires major dismantling of the engine and is almost certainly beyond the scope of the inexperienced owner.

Later engines use a standard lip-seal in a housing; these are much easier to replace and generally do not give the same problems as the old rope type. In either case, leaks from this seal are generally minor and cause little more than a drip beneath the flywheel housing. A seal can often drip for years without giving any major problems, although once the leak is detected it needs careful monitoring to ensure that it is not getting significantly worse.

All leaks should be attended to at the first convenient opportunity, which would usually be at the end of the season when the boat was about to be laid up, and should not therefore interrupt the season's use of the boat. In fact it would not do any harm to leave it for several seasons if it did not appear to be getting any worse, and an oil-absorbent pad beneath the engine will keep the compartment clean.

CHAPTER 5

Cooling Systems

Cooling marine engines can be accomplished using either air or water. Air cooling is generally only suitable for small capacity engines that do not develop large amounts of power (and therefore heat), and is particularly useful on the inland waterways where weeds and rubbish can quickly block a water inlet strainer causing a water-cooled engine to overheat. With air cooling the only requirement is to provide an adequate supply of cool fresh air, and the engine will happily run at a reasonable temperature.

It must be stressed that only engines designed and properly equipped for air cooling can be used as such, because they will have been designed with ducting and finned flywheels to promote a rapid flow of air around the hotspots of the block. The size of the air-intake vents makes it difficult to achieve a very quiet engine installation, and the use of a dry exhaust also contributes to the noise. However, in areas of heavy water pollution the simple air-cooled engine has a lot to offer in terms of ease of maintenance and lack of corrosion.

Today, modern engines are almost universally water-cooled using heat exchangers or keel cooling to ensure that only clean water with added corrosion inhibitors is circulated through the engine block. The addition of anti-freeze and corrosion inhibitors to the water ensures that the internal water passages of the engine have year-round protection.

Raw water cooling takes the water straight out of the river or sea to circulate through the block, and is still used on some petrol engines; it is mainly installed in imported American sports boats that were originally destined for freshwater lake use. The corrosion and cold running problems that raw water cooling generates, particularly in salt water, make it less attractive except where the very lowest initial costs are necessary.

DIRECT OR RAW WATER COOLING

The main difference between fresh water and raw water cooled engines is that there is no header tank or heat exchanger fitted to these engines. Direct cooling that takes raw water directly from the sea or river, circulates it round the engine block and finally discharges it overboard – usually via the exhaust pipework – is a cheap, short-term solution to engine cooling and there are many drawbacks to the system. Particularly important is the problem of running temperature. It is not possible to use a standard thermostat to allow the engine to run at its correct temperature of around 80°C, as this will eventually cause severe blockages to the water passages from impurities and silt building up on the walls of the cooling system passages.

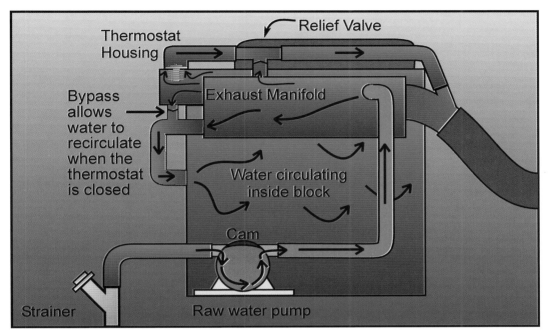

Schematic layout of a typical raw water cooling system.

The usual recommended working temperature for a direct-cooled engine is around 54°C, and this causes minor sludging of the oil as it can never achieve its optimum working temperature; the result of this is increased engine wear. The low temperature also means that items such as calorifiers for domestic water heating do not work as effectively as with freshwater cooling, but the last and most important point is that corrosion products from the hot raw water are continually attacking the engine internals as it impossible to add inhibitors to the water. The entire cooling system must also be drained during the winter months to prevent damage from freezing, as anti-freeze cannot be added other than during the lay-up period due to the lack of a header tank.

Raw water cooling equipment will usually consist of an impeller-type water pump and water-cooled manifold plus a marine gearbox, either mechanical or hydraulic, and a gearbox oil cooler if required.

INDIRECT OR FRESHWATER COOLING

None of the above-mentioned problems occur with indirectly cooled engines, which have a separate freshwater supply from a header tank that provides clean water to the engine block in the manner for which the engine was designed. This means that anti-freeze and corrosion inhibitors can be added to the freshwater supply, preventing the problems that beset raw water-cooled engines. They can also use a standard thermostat and run at their proper designed temperature for maximum efficiency and long life, while also supplying free hot water

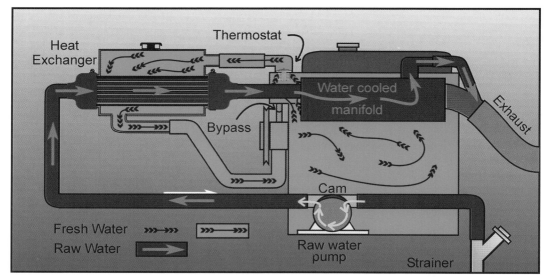

The much preferred freshwater cooling system.

for the galley from a calorifier if required. The relatively modest extra cost is therefore well worth considering. Additional equipment required for indirect cooling includes a heat exchanger (often combined with the water-cooled manifold) and an engine oil cooler if required.

THE HEAT EXCHANGER

Heat exchangers, which on many engines are combined with the water-cooled exhaust manifold to make a neater installation, perform the same function as the

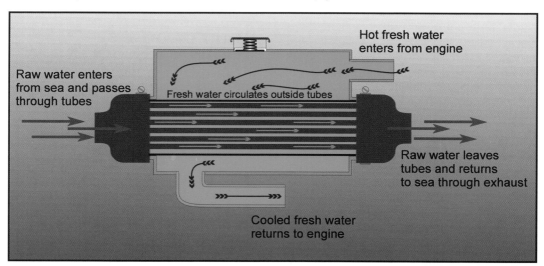

Inside a heat exchanger.

radiator in a vehicle by cooling the water flowing round the engine block. With a radiator it is air, forced through the matrix by either the forward motion of the car or the engine fan that removes the excess heat, but with a heat exchanger it is raw water (drawn in from the sea or river by the raw water pump) that removes the excess heat. It does this by circulating the freshwater (the water in the block) around a tightly packed tube stack in the heat exchanger body. The raw water passes through the tubes and absorbs the heat before entering the exhaust and being discharged overboard back into the sea.

The tube stack is similar to that found in a steam-engine boiler, although the tubes in the heat exchanger are more tightly packed to give maximum cooling effect. The ends of the tube stack are sealed to prevent raw water mixing with the fresh, making it possible to add anti-freeze and anti-corrosives to the system to keep the engine block in tip-top condition. It is important to have a reliable raw-water inlet filter, as the tubes can quickly become clogged if mud and weed are allowed to reach them. Part of the annual service should be to clean out the tubes by gently rodding through with a suitable piece of stiff wire, such as the trusty wire coat-hanger that finds many other uses in the toolbox!

For repair or replacement the complete stack is removable. The ends of the stack are revealed by removing the end covers from the heat exchanger, which will be either a neoprene type secured with hose clips or a metal plate with an 'O'-ring seal secured with bolts. Combined heat-exchanger manifolds used on smaller engines directly replace the old exhaust manifold, while the larger single-unit heat exchanger usually bolts on to the front of the engine and may require additional support brackets.

WATER-COOLED EXHAUST MANIFOLDS

Vehicle exhausts are cooled by air, but as anyone who has accidentally touched one after a run will know, they still become extremely hot! Without the air's cooling influence they would be quite capable of starting a fire, hence the need for water cooling in marine installations. The manifold itself is fairly simple in construction, consisting of a water jacket surrounding an internal tube manifold, which keeps the temperature down to acceptable levels where there is no fire risk.

The photo (overleaf) shows the water-cooled exhaust manifold on the Bedford that we met earlier. (The two tubes running along the front of the manifold are the inlet and outlet for the calorifier, and not part of the manifold.)

It is possible to fabricate a manifold at home using only basic welding skills, although care is needed when aligning the mounting flanges otherwise exhaust leaks will occur. As these manifolds are not particularly expensive to buy it may not be worth the time and trouble to make. Combined heat-exchanger manifolds are very much more precise and are beyond the skills of the DIY enthusiast due to the intricacy of the tube stack.

The water-cooled manifold is a direct replacement for the original exhaust manifold and bolts straight into place. On engines where both the inlet and exhaust manifolds are on the same side it is often necessary to remove the inlet manifold and refit it upside down to provide clearance for the exhaust manifold to fit. On other engines a replacement marine inlet

A typical water-cooled exhaust manifold.

manifold is required, and of course on engines produced specifically for marine use the whole package is designed to fit from the outset.

OIL COOLER

This is a smaller version of the heat exchanger with a tube stack through which the cooling water passes. Engine oil taken via a special adaptor (usually at the oil filter block) is pumped around the tubes and cooled. There are fewer tubes in the oil cooler as the oil does not require the same degree of cooling as the circulating water in the heat exchanger; indeed, if the oil is overcooled the problem of sludging and reduced lubricating efficiency can occur.

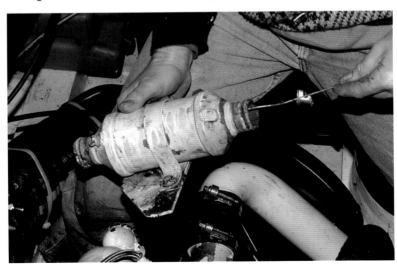

An oil cooler in the process of being cleaned.

RAW WATER PUMP

These pumps are almost universally of the flexible impeller type, being very reliable and powerful for their size. As the name implies, they are fitted on the raw water side of the cooling system, whether it is raw or freshwater cooled. On freshwater-cooled systems this pump is fitted in addition to the standard engine circulating pump used to circulate the water within the engine on freshwater-cooled engines. They are used to draw in cooling water from the river or sea for heat exchanger, exhaust manifold and oil-cooling purposes. Jabsco is the most famous name for this type of pump, and has in fact become the generic term for flexible impeller pumps in the same way that 'Hoover' is the standard name for vacuum cleaners.

There is a wide range of pump types to suit all engines in the marine leisure and light commercial field. Older types and those for slow-revving engines used plain bearings with greasers and adjustable glands, but the majority in service today use roller bearings that are lubricated for life, thereby cutting down on maintenance.

Several different drive methods are available; the simplest is to fit a pulley on to the pump and drive from an additional pulley on the front of the engine crankshaft. The pump is simply mounted on a bracket, which is bolted to the engine. Other types drive from a take-off in the engine timing case and are mounted directly on the engine in place of a blanking plate or some other piece of equipment such as a brake compressor, which is not required on the marine version of the engine.

For certain applications, high speed types drive directly from the engine circulating water pump pulley. With this type the pump body is prevented from spinning by either the fitting of a torque arm or by the pipework itself. This torque arm must be carefully designed so that it does not apply any side loadings on the pump bearing, which would otherwise lead to premature bearing failure. For this reason it is often better to rely on the flexible pipework (*see overleaf below*), which cannot load the bearings.

Whatever the drive type, they all use neoprene impellers to pump the water, so care must be exercised to ensure that they never run dry, as this leads to rapid impeller failure (in a matter of minutes). For this reason it is sensible practice to keep a spare impeller on board. It is also good practice to remove the impeller when

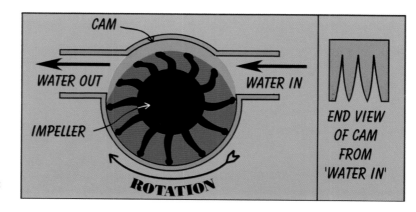

Raw water impeller pumps are the standard cooling pump on 99 per cent of modern engines.

A simple pulley drive pump.

laying up at the end of the season to pre-vent it freezing into place or permanently distorting. The direction of flow of the pump depends on engine rotation and is usually marked on the front cover plate of the pump. This should be noted when planning the pipework layout.

KEEL AND TANK COOLING

Keel cooling was quite popular years ago but is seen less often nowadays. By run-ning heavy cooling pipes along the outside of the bottom of the hull the engine circu-

A high-speed pump mounted on the engine internal water pump and using the flexible hoses as the torque arm.

Keel cooling is rarely used today, but is ideal for heavily polluted waters.

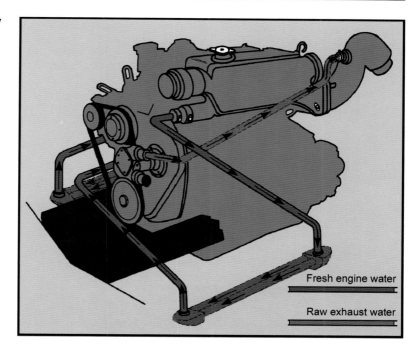

Fresh engine water

Raw exhaust water

lating water is cooled by the flow of river or sea water passing round the pipes. This system is particularly useful in waters that suffer from excessive rubbish pollution as there is no intake strainer to be blocked. A dry exhaust system is necessary unless provision is made to draw in water just for exhaust cooling, but this means the problem of rubbish blocking the strainer is still present. The main problem is that the outside pipework is prone to damage from hitting underwater obstructions, which then requires the boat to be slipped for repair.

Tank cooling is occasionally used on steel boats where a false bottom is welded into the bilge, through which engine cooling water is circulated; it is cooled by heat transference through the bottom of the boat into the water outside. The same considerations for cooling the exhaust are required as for keel cooling, but the problem of damage to underwater pipework is removed. A large

tank area is needed to make the system work efficiently, but it is ideally suited to the needs of narrowboat owners on the inland waterways.

It is sometimes possible simply to utilize the natural water flow and the engine circulating pump to circulate the water in a tank-cooling system, but where the bilge and tank is far below the level of the engine an additional flexible impeller pump is required to ensure satisfactory flow. Whether or not to have a water-cooled exhaust also arises with this system, as there is no water intake in the same way as with a raw water or heat exchanger cooled system. A dry exhaust will tend to be noisier than a water-cooled type, and will also need to be carefully lagged to prevent the high temperatures within the pipe scorching or igniting surrounding timbers, or injuring unsuspecting crew members. However, with a water-cooled exhaust the

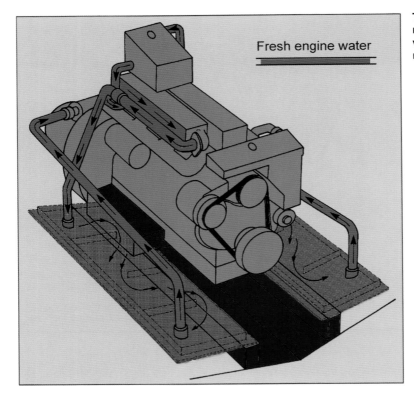

Tank cooling is a rarity, but is still used very occasionally on narrowboats.

Fresh engine water

problems mentioned with the dry system do not occur, although it is essential to arrange a warning system for over-heating as a blockage in the water inlet could go unnoticed until the exhaust became dangerously hot, and in the case of rubber exhaust hose will melt in the extremes of temperature.

1. Once the hoses have been detached there are four bolts securing the heat exchanger to this engine block.

2. With the bolts removed the whole thing can be lifted out for examination and easy cleaning.

3. This Bowman heat exchanger is combined with the exhaust manifold and has a removable tube stack that is accessed after removing the rubber end caps.

4. Although in generally clean condition, some tubes (arrowed) had become blocked with marine detritus. Cleaning every three years or so ensures any blockages are removed before flow is seriously reduced.

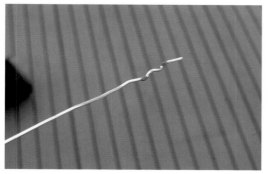

5. An unwound wire coat-hanger is an ideal tool for running through the tubes as the spiral section provides a smooth scraping action.

6. It is important to clean each tube individually, but it is worth the effort to keep the system flowing freely.

7. Flush the tubes through with clean water, and also flush the heat-exchanger body in order to remove any residue from the latter.

8. Refit the heat-exchanger end caps, reinstall the heat exchanger on to the engine, and reconnect the pipework.

SERVICING FRESHWATER ENGINE COOLING SYSTEMS

Tube Stack Cleaning

See the photos on pp. 70–71. Heat exchangers, oil coolers and intercoolers come in many designs, so the method of dismantling prior to cleaning the stacks will vary slightly between engines. The cooler in the photo top right on p. 71 is a Cummins heat exchanger with a separate header tank, and is relatively easy to remove for cleaning. It is just possible to clean the tube stacks while it is in place, but a much better job can be made with it removed.

Intercooler Stack Cleaning

See the photos below. It is not always necessary to completely remove the intercooler, but on this occasion one of the bottom cover plate-holding bolts was too stiff to free off with it in place, so it had to come off.

1. The top and bottom plates usually need to be removed to allow the tube stack to be removed by pushing it through from one end.

2. Once removed, the stack can be examined and any problems corrected. A couple of tube ends have been damaged by something hard passing through the system, while others are blocked by what looks like cooked prawn!

3. The trusty wire coat-hanger again proves its worth for cleaning the tubes. It also gently straightened the damaged tube ends.

4. Clean the tube end covers and refit the seals before fitting the cover plates.

Renewing Pencil Anodes

See photos below and at top of p. 74. Pencil anodes (where fitted) protect the internal passageways of the raw water side of a freshwater-cooled engine. They are fitted in the heat exchanger, intercooler and water-cooled manifold. They have a relatively short life as they are subjected to hot, fast-flowing water and usually need changing at least once a season, sometimes more often.

Oil Cooler Stack Cleaning

See photos on p. 76 middle and bottom. The last items requiring tube cleaning are the engine and gearbox oil coolers. If they can be cleaned without disconnecting the oil pipes this saves additional work.

Raw Water Pump

See the photos on pp. 75–78. The raw water pump should be an annual service item but the one pictured had been neglected for several years and was overdue for checking and service. I always carry a complete spare pump for emergency use as it is generally far quicker to change the pump than to try to change the impeller at sea. In this case the pump is located behind the engine

1. Pencil anodes need to be checked for wear and replaced where necessary, usually every year.

2. Unscrew and discard the worn anode section . . .

3. . . . and replace it with a new one, having first applied a little water-resistant grease to the thread.

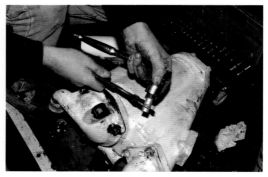

4. Tighten the two pieces with grips and a spanner.

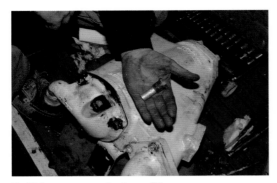

5. It is now ready to refit.

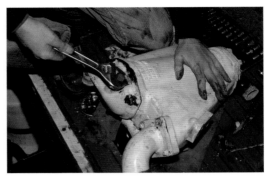

6. Apply a little more water-resistant grease to the thread of the fitting, and tighten it in position. Renewing pencil anodes is a similar procedure, whatever the piece of equipment they are protecting.

1. If the oil cooler can be cleaned without disconnecting the oil pipes it saves additional work and mess.

2. This small Bowman engine oil cooler is easily cleaned *in situ* once the rubber end caps are removed.

3. In case you are thinking that tube stack cleaning is not something worth bothering with, you might like to consider this fifteen-year-old oil cooler stack that was never cleaned until the engine over-heated to near seizure point!

1. Some pumps are awkwardly positioned, which makes it even more important to carry a complete spare.

2. With the pump off the engine, the first task is to remove the cover plate.

3. Lift off the cover and gasket or, as in this case, the ring seal.

4. Check the inside of the cover for wear. If it is excessive the cover can be fitted inside out to provide a new surface for the impeller to seal against. Before fitting in this way ensure the outer face is clean and that there are no sharp, raised edges around the bolt holes.

5. Before removing the impeller check which way the blades are sitting to help with reassembly.

6. Remove the impeller end cover by carefully prising it off with a flat-bladed screwdriver.

7. Use a proper impeller puller to draw out the impeller: don't use screwdrivers to prise it out, as that will definitely damage the impeller, and will probably also damage the inner edges of the pump itself.

8. With the impeller removed, check for wear in the bottom of the pump body. Many pumps have a separate wear plate in the bottom that can be reversed in the same way as the pump cover.

9. Just to prove that it is not a good idea to ignore the pump at service time, this split shows that the impeller is close to breaking up and should have been replaced several years ago.

10. Before fitting the new impeller (or refitting the old one if it is still in good condition), liberally grease the inside to ensure it will come out easily next time.

11. If the impeller has a separate woodruff key, grease this at the same time.

12. Give the impeller blades a liberal wash with soapy water to ease insertion into the pump body.

13. Insert the impeller into the pump, turning it while pushing it home in order to align the blades in the correct orientation, as was established prior to removal.

14. If a woodruff key is used, slide it into the slot between the impeller and drive shaft.

15. Refit the impeller end cover. This is an important item, as some pumps will not prime if this is left out.

16. If a ring seal is used, clean the groove prior to refitting. If a gasket is used, clean the mating faces and use a new one.

17. It is a good idea to use a little grease in the ring-seal groove to keep it in position while the face plate is fitted.

18. Clean the face plate inner surface before refitting.

19. Make sure the pump mounting gasket is in good condition, or fit a new one. When refitting the pump make sure it is the right way up, with outlet and inlet in the correct orientation!

chaincase and is quite awkward to get at. Thankfully it is secured with two bolts that are quick to remove, and the whole thing can be replaced within ten minutes.

Pump Connections

When using a spare pump as the quick-change standby it is important to be able to remove the hoses quickly and easily. Marine-reinforced hose, which is used to avoid collapse under pump suction, hardens over time and often the only way to disconnect it is to cut it off and renew it. This is clearly of no use where the pump needs to be changed quickly.

Where it is essential to use convoluted hose for the main hose run, make up an end connection using a copper tube stub 4 or 5in (10 or 12cm) long in the appropriate

size to fit inside the hose. The end of the convoluted hose is warmed slightly in hot water to soften it, and the copper tube is secured halfway into the tube with two hose clips for a permanent fix. Then use a 4in (10cm) length of vehicle hose on the exposed end of the copper, again secured with two hose clips. This hose is used to make the final connection on to the pump with a single hose clip, and ensures it can be fitted and removed very easily while still providing a reliable seal every time.

This hose connector arrangement shown below has been in place for several years,

A reliable hose end connector, allowing quick pump removal.

This one has been in use for several years and is consistently dependable.

but still comes off easily and forms a perfect, secure seal when refitted. It doesn't take very long to make up, but is worth the effort when the pump has to be disconnected in a hurry.

Thermostats

Thermostats are often forgotten but they can eventually go wrong, and usually in the closed position, which means the engine rapidly overheats. Less serious is when they fail in the open position, as the engine simply never reaches its correct operating temperature. The quickest cure for a closed thermostat when away from home is to simply remove it and fit a replacement at the next convenient port of call. For an open thermostat simply keep a careful eye on the engine temperature to ensure that the thermostat doesn't decide to close. Again, replace it at the next convenient point.

Test the thermostat by placing it in a pan of hot water and watching to see when it opens. As long as it opens before the water boils you can assume it is all right. For a more accurate test, place a thermometer in the water and check the temperature when the thermostat opens. Thermostats can be mounted in various ways, but generally

Refill the system with a 50/50 mixture of good quality antifreeze/corrosion inhibitor.

speaking they are easy to get at and can be removed and replaced by removing the housing, lifting the old one out and fitting the new one. Fit a new gasket to ensure the housing doesn't leak after replacement. Once everything has been reconnected, the heat exchanger system must be refilled with a 50-50 mixture of good quality antifreeze and water, and the level rechecked after the engine has run up to temperature and cooled again.

Belts

See the photos overleaf. Drive belts, whether for pumps or alternators, need to be checked at least annually during the main service. Pump drive belts are particularly important, as a failure will cause drastic overheating. There are several different types of belt, from notched vee to 'poly-vee'. Whatever the type, it needs to be carefully checked for wear and damage and replaced if there is any doubt about its condition.

On engines such as Cummins that use poly-vee belts, the belt tension is achieved using a spring-loaded idler pulley. Tension is released using a 3/8 square drive ratchet in the square hole on the idler arm to allow the belt to be replaced.

To remove the thermostat, undo the cover holding bolts and lift it off. The thermostat can then be lifted out.

1. If the belts are protected by a cover this needs to be removed first.

2. Poly-vee belts are flat with ridges running their length, giving them a high degree of grip.

3. Using a 3/8 square drive ratchet to release belt tension when changing a Poly-vee belt.

4. Fitting a tight vee belt over the lip of the pulley before turning the engine to roll it into place.

With standard 'vee' belts, when fitting a new one it is sometimes a little on the short side and the trick to getting it on to the pulleys is to place it round the crank-shaft pulley and then push it as far on to the alternator (or pump) pulley as possible. Then while holding the belt in position, turn the engine over with a spanner on the crankshaft pulley nut, and the belt will roll into place. It can then be tensioned in the normal manner.

Water Strainers

See the photos opposite. Raw water strainers need to be checked on a regular basis, especially if cruising in shallow waters. These are the first line of defence against sediment and weed blocking the engine-cooling system, yet all they need is a quick flush out with clean water to keep them clear. High level strainers mounted above the waterline mean there is no need to close the sea-cock before removing the cover for cleaning. It also makes rodding through an easy task. When refitting the cover, give the seal a light smear of grease to help it bed down and form a watertight seal. If a perfect seal is not made, the pump will not be able to prime the system and draw water through.

1. A clean strainer basket is the first line of defence for the cooling system.

2. Here the strainers are mounted under a hatch in the saloon well above the waterline where they are convenient for quick access.

3. Make sure the pipework to the strainer is not partially blocked by rodding it through after cleaning the strainer basket.

4. Check the cover seal is in good condition, and give it a light greasing to help it seal when the cover is refitted.

5. If a straight down connection to the skin fittings can be arranged there is less chance of a blockage occurring in the pipe, and rodding through becomes very easy.

RAW WATER PUMP OVERHAUL

Jabsco is the largest manufacturer of flexible impeller pumps with a worldwide network of dealers carrying a comprehensive range of spares and impeller kits, so the owner of any type of vessel fitted with a Jabsco pump can be totally self-sufficient when away from the home port. This is an important consideration with any onboard equipment, particularly when long-distance cruising. Jabsco's catalogue lists engines, past and present, for which standard pumps or parts are available, and it also contains an informative section on correct pump installation practice. This is important in order to avoid premature failure – especially of bearings – which can occur with either belt- or shaft-driven pumps.

As with all engineering, the secret of a long reliable life is good installation practice, and a little extra time spent ensuring that the pump and drive are properly mounted and aligned will ensure a long, trouble-free life. On belt-driven pumps this means ensuring that the pulleys are accurately aligned. On gear-driven pumps the clearance between the driving and driven gear teeth may be important, while on high speed pumps it is essential that the torque arm is properly mounted so as to prevent side loads on the bearing.

There are basically three different types of shaft seal used on Jabsco pumps, depending on pump model and type. The simplest is the traditional gland packing used on pumps with plain bearings; it is not generally used on modern marine engines as the gland needs to drip slightly to keep the packing moist, and the high speed of modern engines tends to wear the packing and the bearings.

The lip seal and mechanical seal are the most common types used on modern marine engines, and both have their advantages. The mechanical seal, which consists of a carbon ring rotating against a stationary ceramic seat, has the advantage that it never wears the pump shaft, but these are more critical to assemble and can cause problems for the amateur working on his own boat without suitable assembly tools.

The lip seal, which many people are more familiar with in other applications, is straightforward to assemble on to the pump, but causes gradual shaft wear. However, most Jabsco pumps incorporate a small spacer known as a 'wear plate', which can be removed when shaft wear is detected. This allows a new seal to be positioned further into the pump on an unworn portion of the shaft, thereby doubling the life of the shaft.

The following basic principles apply to all makes of flexible impeller pump.

Flexible Impeller Pumps

In the photograph opposite above are the three most common types of engine-cooling impeller pump; from left to right: Jabsco 29500 flange-mounted, shaft drive; Jabsco 22940 water pump-mounted, high speed; and the Jabsco 52080 foot-mounted universal, pulley drive.

High Speed Pumps (Jabsco 22940)

See the photos on pp. 83–86. Having removed the impeller as seen in the previous servicing section, the first job when dismantling the pump for overhaul is to remove the cam. To replace the mechanical-type seal, the circlip, which secures the bearing housing, must be removed and this is accessible through the cutaways in the rear of the bearing housing. Once the circlip is freed from its slot, the bearing housing is tapped firmly with a soft-faced mallet

Three common Jabsco pump types: 29500 flange mount, shaft drive; 22940 high speed, pump mount; 52080 foot mount, pulley drive.

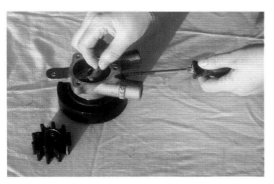

1. Remove the cam.

2. Remove the bearing housing circlip.

3. Use a soft-faced mallet to separate the bearing, housing, shaft and ceramic half of the mechanical seal from the body.

4. Separate the two halves.

5. Lift the ceramic half of the seal off the shaft.

7. Clean the pump of salt and surface corrosion before reassembly.

6. Knock out and discard the carbon face half of the seal.

to separate the bearing, housing, shaft and ceramic (stationary) half of the mechanical seal from the pump body. Once free, the two halves can be separated.

The ceramic half of the seal is now exposed and can be lifted off the shaft.

Note: On the larger Jabsco 22740 high-speed pump the bearing is a press fit on to the spigot on the pump body and must be pressed off rather than tapped.

The carbon face half of the seal is tapped out of the pump body and discarded, as it will almost certainly be damaged during removal. At this point the pump is completely dismantled and may be cleaned of salt and surface corrosion before reassembly begins.

Note: If it is necessary to renew the bearing, the housing should be slowly heated in an oven until the bearing can be *gently* tapped out. It should never be pressed out cold because the housing is shrunk on to the bearing during initial assembly and will be damaged. When renewing a bearing in this way it is possible that the housing will become distorted. It may therefore be safer to order a new bearing and housing assembly complete.

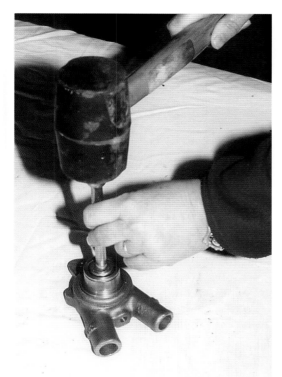

8. Fit the new carbon face half of the mechanical seal.

9. Slide the ceramic half of the seal on to the shaft, and push the pump body and bearing housing together before refitting the circlip.

10. Refit the cam.

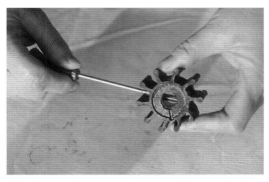

11. Ensure the pin is screwed through the impeller, with no protrusion at either end.

12. Install the lightly greased impeller, turning it to bend the vanes into the pump body.

13. Fit a new gasket to maintain the correct running tolerances.

14. Refit the cover, or renew if worn on both sides.

15. Evenly tighten the securing screws.

Reassembly

Reassembly of the pump is a reversal of the dismantling procedure and begins with the renewal of the carbon face half of the mechanical seal, which should be a snug push fit within the pump body. The final location of the seal half must be made with either a smooth-ended tube of suitable size used as a drift or, better still, a press.

Note: A suitably sized socket and long bar makes an ideal smooth-ended drift, but as these carbon seals are so fragile before installation it is better to seek the services of the local engineers to insert this half of the seal. This is one of only two areas where the DIY owner is likely to find a problem with pump servicing.

The ceramic half of the seal is slid on to the shaft and the face smeared with a light oil to provide lubrication on initial start-up. The pump body and bearing housing can then be pushed together and lightly tapped home and the circlip refitted. Lightly tapping the circlip with a screwdriver and hammer ensures it is securely located in the groove.

The cam is fitted next, with a generous coat of gasket sealant on the face to prevent any air passing round the back of the cam and causing priming difficulties on initial start-up. Before finally tightening the cam screw, lightly tap the edge of the cam to ensure that it is flush with the face of the pump body, otherwise the front cover may not sit flush on the face, causing leaks.

Note: Ensure that the cam fixing screw is of the correct length and does not protrude above the cam face, otherwise the impeller will be severely damaged as soon as the engine is started.

When fitting a new pin drive impeller such as is used with this pump it is important to ensure that the pin is screwed through the impeller with no protrusion at either end to avoid it damaging the impeller vanes. Before installing the impeller, lightly grease the inside of the pump body and the impeller itself to assist initial pump priming. Turn the impeller while fitting to bend the vanes into the pump body. It is important to refit the gasket to maintain the correct running tolerances. It is permissible to fabricate a new gasket from plain brown paper if a proper replacement is not available.

If the cover plate shows signs of excessive wear it may be installed inside out to ensure that the correct running tolerances are maintained. This one (opposite top right) has been worn on both sides, as evidenced by the words and numbers within the wear area, and must be replaced. The securing screws should be evenly tightened, being careful not to overtighten them as they will snap if overstressed. This is particularly important on older pumps and very small models, where the screw size is minimal. It is good practice to renew the screws whenever the pump is serviced.

Flange-Mounting Pumps
(Jabsco 29500)

This pump is the current replacement model for the ubiquitous Perkins 4108 pump, and includes a multi-blade impeller. It uses two bearings separated by a spacer in order to give a longer bearing life by spreading

2. The cam is then removed in the normal manner, followed by the wear plate.

the loading over a wider area. The bearings are lubricated by engine oil as they are open to the engine timing cover and receive oil from the timing gears supply.

Remove the cover and gasket in the usual way. This impeller is spline-driven, and a spline seal is fitted over the end of the spline to prevent sand or grit damaging the spline itself. Lift this off before removing the impeller, and refit it on reassembly. The cam is then removed. There is a wear plate (the false bottom already mentioned) fitted behind the impeller, and this is located on a lug to prevent it rotating. This is lifted out once the impeller and cam have been removed. An 'O'-ring seal is located

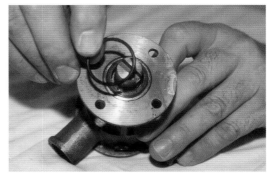

1. With the cover and gasket removed, the seal can be lifted off.

3. Remove the 'O'-ring seal.

4. The shaft and bearing assembly are pressed out towards the mounting flange.

6. Remove the 'slinger' fitted between the seals.

in a groove on the back of the pump and is next removed.

The shaft and bearing assembly are pressed out towards the mounting flange; a large bench vice and sockets from a socket set of the appropriate size can be used. If neither is available the local engineers will be able to press them out for you. The spigot that carries the 'O' ring will be pressed out along with the bearings. A 'slinger' is fitted between the seals and is a very important safety feature, because in the event of the water seal leaking it throws the water outwards and prevents it from running along the shaft and creeping under the bearing oil seal from the non-pressure side, as this would damage the bearings and contaminate the engine oil. Remove it by pulling it out after the shaft has been removed.

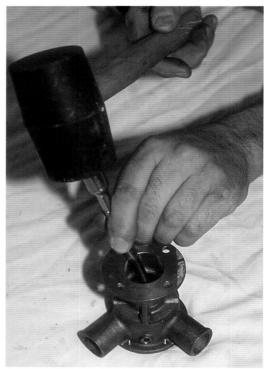

5. The spigot that carries the 'O' ring is pressed out along with the bearings.

7. The lip seals are tapped out next.

8. The pump is now dismantled and can be cleaned of salts and corrosion.

9. Press the seals firmly into place with the lip towards the pressure side.

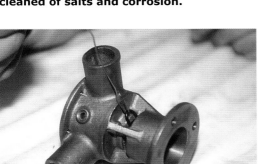

10. Slip the 'slinger' into the opening between the two seals prior to refitting the shaft and bearing assembly.

The lip seals are tapped out next. There are two seals in this type of pump, one for engine oil and the other for water. The engine oil seal prevents the oil in the timing cover from escaping while lubricating the pump bearings. The water seal prevents water leaking from the pump body.

The pump is now dismantled and can be cleaned of salts and corrosion.

Reassembly
Note: The bearings are an interference fit on the shaft, and if replacement is required they must be pressed off the shaft along with the spacer. A large bench vice and suitably sized tube or socket will do the job

in the same manner as was used to press the bearings out of the pump body.

The new bearings are then fitted using either a tubular drift on the bearing centre journal or a press. Again, this may be another job for the local engineering shop.

To replace the seals, each is firmly pressed into place with the lip towards the pressure side. This means that the open side of the water seal with the spring visible around the inner lip should be facing the impeller, and the open side of the oil seal should be facing the engine, so that the seals are actually back to back. The 'slinger' is slipped into the opening between the two seals prior to refitting the shaft and bearing assembly, which is then pressed into position. If the wear plate is found to have excessive wear it may be reversed in the same way as the cover plate already mentioned. Once this is replaced, reassembly is exactly the same as described for the high-speed pump.

Note: Although we have only covered two particular pumps in this feature, between the two, the details are similar for all other pumps in the range as well as all other makes.

There is an impeller kit available for every Jabsco pump in the range, and it is

There is an impeller kit available for every Jabsco pump in the range, and it is sensible to keep at least one on board as part of the on-board spares kit.

sensible to keep at least one on board as part of the on-board spares kit.

WINTER PROTECTION

It is during the winter months that the most extensive (and expensive) damage may take place on board craft that are left unattended. And it is often the engine that suffers the greatest – although with a few simple and timely precautions all these problems can be avoided. The most obvious is to fill the freshwater cooling system with a good quality anti-freeze. The best

kinds are those that can be left in the system all year round, and which offer corrosion protection as well as anti-freeze properties. If this is changed every couple of years at the end of the season when the oil is changed it will help to keep the engine in tip-top condition throughout the year.

Naturally this can only be achieved with freshwater-cooled engines, although it is possible to introduce anti-freeze into a raw-water-cooled engine system. As there is no header tank to fill in the manner of freshwater-cooled engines, the engine water inlet is disconnected from the inlet strainer and the hose placed in a large bucket of 50/50 anti-freeze and water mixture. The engine is then briefly run to circulate the mixture through the system and as soon as it starts appearing from the exhaust the engine is stopped. The water inlet is then reconnected to the strainer ready for the following season.

If anti-freeze is not used in a raw water-cooled engine it must be drained down before leaving for the winter. However, draining down may not protect the engine from freezing damage, as pockets of water are often left which cannot be drained, therefore by running anti-freeze solution through the engine these pockets of water will be flushed through and the mixture will remain. Boats with raw water-cooled engines used on rivers and canals are particularly at risk from freezing damage as freshwater freezes at a higher temperature than salt water.

Replacing Expansion (Core) Plugs
See the pictures on pp. 91–93. Should the worst happen and the engine freeze solid, it is to be hoped that the built-in expansion plugs (or core plugs, as they are sometimes known) will do their job and be forced out as the freezing water expands into ice. This is what they are designed for, but in very

severe conditions the rate of freezing may be too great to allow even expansion of the ice, and the result is a cracked block: if it can be repaired at all, it means the engine must be removed from the boat and totally stripped down for welding.

This is an expensive and time-consuming task that can be easily avoided by early precautionary measures. From the foregoing it is easy to understand the important role that the humble expansion plug performs. Unfortunately the light construction

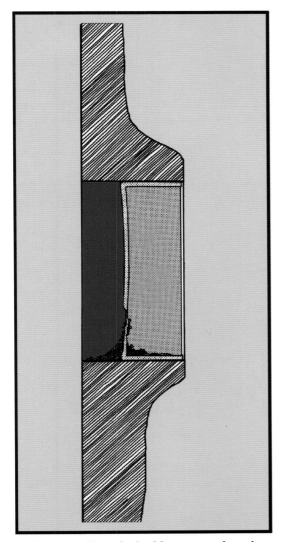

1. Cross-section of a leaking expansion plug.

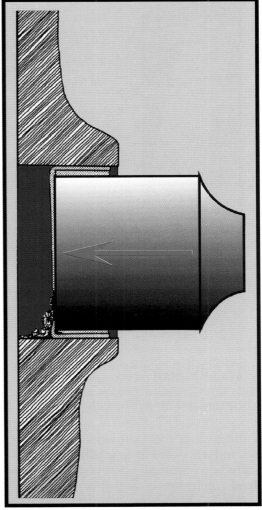

2. Loosen it by using a suitable drift to knock it in slightly.

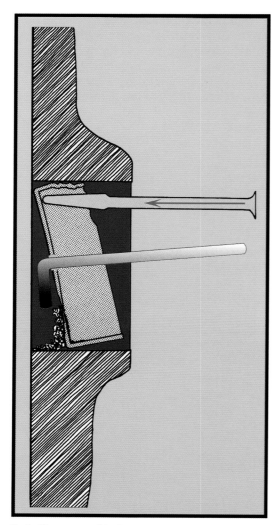

3. Drill a central hole and slip a hook through to prevent the plug falling inside the block. Use a small chisel to turn the plug, allowing it to be gripped for pulling out.

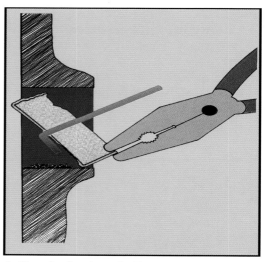

4. Use the hook and pliers to remove the plug.

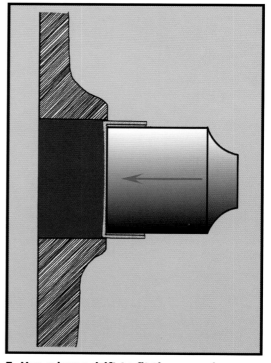

5. Use a large drift to fit the new plug.

of these plugs makes them a prime target for corrosion, and in time they will eventually begin to leak, at which point they should be replaced.

This is normally a straightforward job, except where the plug is situated in an inaccessible position, such as behind the

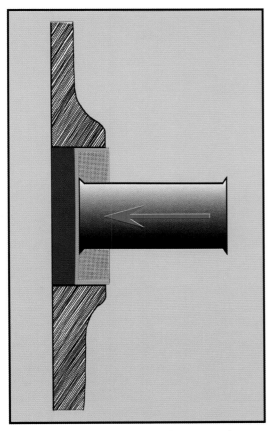

6. Once it is nearly in position, complete the fitting with a smaller drift in the centre to expand the plug.

flywheel. In this case the gearbox will need to be removed, followed by the flywheel housing and flywheel before replacement can take place. In this case a temporary repair can often be achieved by using one of the leak remedies that are poured into the cooling system, and plug the gap from the inside.

Happily the rest of the plugs are more accessible, and replacement does not take long. Each plug is in the form of a dished cup and is an interference fit in its bore; they are generally in stock sizes, and can

be bought in sets from most car accessory shops. To remove the old plug it should be lightly tapped inwards to break the seal of corrosion and sediment deposits, which will have built up over a long period.

Care must be taken to ensure that the plug is not tapped right into the block, or an interesting half hour will be spent trying to fish it out again. To prevent this happening it is a good idea to drill a hole through the centre of the plug and pass a hooked item (such as an Allen key) through the plug. This can also be used to assist in pulling the plug out once it has become free.

Once it begins to move it can be tapped on one side to turn it sideways in its bore, at which point it will be possible to pull it out with either the hook or a pair of pliers. Never attempt to prise it out against the face of the bore, as this will damage the seal surface between the plug and the block and may lead to further leaks.

Once the plug is removed, the bore may be lightly cleaned using fine emery cloth to remove all the old sediment residue. The new plug should be lightly smeared with gasket cement around the outside of the sealing surface, and then lightly tapped into position using the same drift as was used to loosen the old plug. When it is almost home, use a smaller diameter soft drift in the centre of the plug so that the convex surface causes a slight expansion of the seal as it is tapped home, making an effective seal. When the plug is properly located, the seal sides should be flush with the face of the bore in the block.

Should the new plug show tendencies to weep after fitting, this will usually stop after a few hours; if it doesn't, using one of the proprietary cooling system conditioners will cure it, and will also help to prevent future corrosion at the same time, making this a worthwhile part of the cooling system annual service anyway.

CHAPTER 6

Electrical Systems

Electrical systems on boats are particularly vulnerable to the damp and this is especially so on salt water. This makes it essential to ensure that the electrics on marine diesels get extra special care if they are to perform in a safe and reliable manner. Good installation practice is the first step towards a reliable system and this, coupled with regular simple maintenance, makes the difference between trouble-free cruising and endless problems.

BATTERIES

The heart of the boat's electrical system is the battery or batteries, and without these all but the smallest of engines cannot be started. Ideally batteries should be mounted away from the engine compartment in a separate ventilated compartment, however it is usually more convenient to mount them within the engine compartment where leads to starter motors can be as short as possible to provide maximum current for starting with minimal voltage drop.

Safe Battery Installation
Batteries must be securely mounted, and ideally should be contained within a GRP-lined box as the resin is unaffected by battery acid. A plywood box glassed inside with two layers of chopped strand mat and resin is simple to make and provides a secure home for the batteries when bolted down in a suitably ventilated compartment.

It is possible to buy plastic battery boxes from chandlers which are also immune to acid and which incorporate a lid, but these are not available in sizes to suit large batteries and anyway would not be strong enough to give adequate support to the batteries in choppy weather.

Not only must the battery box be strong, but the batteries must also be firmly fixed within the box to prevent them moving about. This can be achieved by providing a lip on the bottom of the box for each battery to sit in, and then bolting a timber strap across the top of the batteries. A lid is important and should be included in home-built battery boxes as it prevents metal items such as spanners falling on top of the batteries and causing a massive short circuit followed by fire, or an explosion in a shower of acid.

It is vital to arrange an efficient ventilation system for batteries mounted in the engine compartment, as standard truck batteries give off relatively large quantities of hydrogen under conditions of heavy charging, which can lead to explosion if contact is made with sparks from unprotected electric motors. It is therefore essential to ensure that all ventilation extractor fans are of the sealed spark-proof type. Sealed-for-life 'leisure' batteries do not gas to the same extent so are a safer although more expensive option.

For the same reason, all electrical equipment should be switched off every time before the battery terminals are disconnected otherwise the small arc as the terminals are lifted could similarly cause an explosion, with quite catastrophic results for the person next to the batteries!

Battery Maintenance

All the terminal connections on batteries and isolating switches should be clean and kept greased with either Vaseline or one of the proprietary battery terminal greases available from motor accessory shops. Battery electrolyte levels should be checked as part of the weekly engine service schedule of oil and water levels, topping up as necessary using deionized water. Any sudden drop in electrolyte level will indicate a damaged battery casing or possibly severe overcharging, causing buckled plates in the battery and irrevocable damage.

Modern low-maintenance batteries should not require topping up more than about once a year, but if an overcharge situation arises even these will need more frequent attention, a clear indication that the entire system needs checking. Maintenance-free batteries (which are, of course, that much more expensive) can almost be fitted and forgotten, but even these need to have their terminals cleaned and greased occasionally.

Batteries deteriorate most rapidly when the boat is laid up throughout the winter and they are left in a discharged state when they may even freeze and split the casing. The very best way to treat the batteries is to charge them fully at the end of the season and then give them a trickle charge top-up every month throughout the lay-up period. If it is not possible to get down to the boat regularly it is best to take the batteries home where they can be properly cared for.

Battery Capacity

Electrical systems on boats range from the extremely simple to the highly complex, depending on the boat and the amount of equipment on board. To ensure the engine always starts when the starter button is pressed it is essential to have a properly designed and reliable charging system. With this fundamental area correctly installed and maintained the rest of the system should not pose any problems. While the charging circuit is the key to an efficient and reliable electrical installation, it is the battery that is the heart of the system and the first point to check is whether it is of sufficient capacity to start the engine. Engine manufacturers provide specific advice on starting battery requirements for their engines, but it will usually need to be of a greater capacity than the battery used for starting the vehicle equivalent of the boat's engine, as this allows for a certain amount of self discharge should the boat be left unused for a long period.

There are several different classifications applying to batteries that all provide the same information in different forms. The easiest to understand in my opinion is the CCA (cold cranking amps) standard. This refers to the maximum amperage available from the battery for starting a cold engine. 1200 amps is about the maximum found on standard truck batteries, with 1000 amps being more common. Either of these is sufficient for starting the average boat diesel engine. Note that some older diesel engines require greater cranking power than their modern counterparts due to the outmoded design of their starter motors, and it is likely that a modern engine will require less battery starting capacity than an older model.

Good quality, heavy-duty commercial vehicle batteries are suitable for boat use and are a lot cheaper than specialist marine

Marine batteries in the foreground and a standard truck battery behind.

Ensure the battery terminals are well greased to avoid corrosion.

A sturdy battery box is essential to keep the batteries safely in position.

batteries. However, they do not have the long life of proper marine batteries, and many people prefer the advantages of the maintenance-free types that are also spill-proof.

There are several types of battery available for special purposes and I have personally found the 'Optima' range of marine batteries to offer very long self-discharge times when not used and plenty of reserve power from a comparatively small case. (The Optima batteries in the foreground of the picture are of higher capacity than the vehicle battery to the rear.) The 'blue top' model shown is for general use including

Regularly check the electrolyte levels in standard truck batteries.

engine starting, while others are deep discharge types that can be discharged much further than standard truck batteries without damage. These are not suitable for engine starting as they are not designed for the sudden large discharge involved, however they will power equipment and accessories for far longer than a truck battery. I personally prefer the general use type. I have owned the one in the picture for over twelve years and it often sits in the shed for a year or more before being used, and will then start an average diesel engine without being previously recharged.

Ensuring Longevity
With the battery size settled there are several steps to be taken to ensure long life. As already discussed, the primary need is for a sturdy battery box in which the batteries can be securely contained. This must be strong enough to hold the batteries safely in place in all weathers, and should ideally have a fitted lid to prevent metal objects dropping on to the terminals. The lid must be ventilated to allow any gases from the charging process to escape, thus preventing dangerous accumulations from building up. A box constructed of $\frac{3}{4}$in (18mm) ply with a fibreglass mat/resin lining to resist acid spills is ideal for the purpose.

The battery terminals will need cleaning and greasing at least once a season, preferably during the lay-up service. The electrolyte level should also be checked and topped up if necessary at least once a month (of course maintenance-free batteries will not require this to be done).

CHARGING

The usual response to the need for greater electrical power in today's modern power cruiser is to install larger batteries, but this simply extends charging time. Engine manufacturers do not often install alternators of sufficient output to charge the large capacity batteries used today; 80 amps is about average. Yet even when a large capacity alternator is installed you can be fairly certain it is fitted with a standard vehicle charging regulator, which is totally unsuited to the electrical needs of today.

Common battery charging problems are sulphation and counter voltage. Sulphation occurs when batteries are left in a discharged state for long periods allowing lead sulphate to build up on the cell plates, resulting in deterioration and untimely failure.

Counter voltage occurs during charging due to charge build-up on the surface of the battery plates before it can coalesce into the cells. This convinces the vehicle regulator that a higher rate of charge has been attained, hence the quick drop from high charge current into even a heavily discharged battery. After a short period of time battery capacity becomes reduced by about 30 per cent when charged using an alternator with a vehicle regulator. This effectively means that the battery is now smaller than when new, but still housed

1. Fit the alternator battery management system control box.

2. Run the wiring through the boat.

3. If necessary, convert the alternator to suit the management system.

4. A standard regulator alongside a (fitted) modified version.

5. Temperature sensors adjust the charge voltage to suit the conditions.

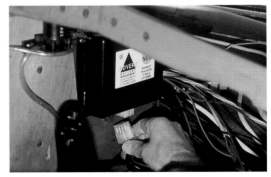

6. Finally, plug the wiring loom into the control box.

in the same case. This is the point where additional batteries are often fitted, instead of solving the real problem of lost capacity. Fitting a specialized battery-sensed type of regulator improves overall charging performance and, equally important, restores some of the battery's lost capacity.

The problem with vehicle regulators is that they firmly set the alternator output to approximately 14.2 volts. This is quite adequate for the simple charging needs of road vehicles, where the lack of temperature compensation means car batteries are undercharged in winter and over-charged in summer, but replacement costs are low – unlike the hefty marine battery!

Vehicle regulators use 'machine sensing' and detect charge voltage at the alternator rather than at the battery. This cheap system is fine on a car, but not a complex marine electrical system that typically includes a split charge system. Unable to sense voltage at the battery, the regulator cannot compensate for losses in the wiring between battery and alternator, or the 0.9 volts customarily lost through standard split charge blocking diodes. With these losses, charge voltage reaching the battery may be reduced to around 13 volts, which is insufficient to overcome counter voltage. The regulator therefore 'thinks' that the battery is fully charged, and cuts the charge to a trickle, leaving that 30 per cent capacity unused.

Specialized regulators often convert the alternator to 'battery sensing' and detect voltage at the battery via an additional lead. They can thus compensate for losses in the wiring and through blocking diodes by adjusting the rate of charge to suit the actual needs of the battery. If battery and alternator capacity are sufficient but charging performance is unsatisfactory, the obvious solution is to ditch the standard regulator and install a specialized version.

My personal choice is the 'Adverc', a development of one of the first to appear on the market over two decades ago and electronically robust. I have used one on my own boat since she was launched twenty-six years ago, yet despite this longevity it is only recently that their value is being recognized. Of particular interest to owners of twin-engine vessels is that one Adverc regulator will control two alternators, either both together or singly when running on one engine. They are now a standard fit on emergency vehicles such as fire engines and ambulances, as well as commercial vehicles with a high battery draw such as tail-lift delivery trucks that constantly use the battery's power with only a short charge between stops.

The most visible effect of fitting an 'Adverc' is the speed with which batteries are recharged. Charge drop-off into heavily discharged batteries doesn't happen, and the batteries charge in about half the time without overcharging or gassing. To ensure the batteries are charged fully and safely, a variable charging cycle is used. This charges at a voltage below the gassing point for the first five minutes, then increases the charging voltage to just above the gassing point, but not for long enough to allow the batteries to actually begin gassing. A 'rest' period of low charging follows, which allows the true state of the battery to be checked before the next period of high charge. This cycle continues until the batteries are fully charged, and then only compensates for current draw while under way.

The visible effect of this monitored charging control can be seen when the batteries are full and there is only a trickle charge being provided. However, switch on several high-current draw items such as engine-room fans and bow thrusters, and the charge rate instantly rises to compensate for the current draw. Temperature compensation via a small temperature sensor mounted adjacent to the batteries means that the rate of charge is increased in cold conditions and reduced in high temperature situations.

'Adverc' is suitable for DIY installation, but for anyone feeling disinclined to install the system themselves, there is a nationwide network of installing dealers. Even so, while other regulators are available, installation is fairly similar for all types and this installation is typical. The first job is to mount the 'Adverc' unit vertically in a dry, protected position with the plug downwards to avoid any possibility of water ingress – in this case, on the partition beside the instrument panel. The most difficult part of the job is running the wiring loom through the boat to the alternators and batteries, and the ease or complexity of this task will vary from boat to boat. The only modification required to the alternator is to exchange the standard regulator for a modified exchange version with an external field connection. This is a simple matter of undoing the two screws, removing the old unit, installing the new modified unit, and securing with the screws.

Alternatively you can modify the standard regulator yourself. The difference between the two regulators is the extra field connection, which is soldered to one of the internal terminals. This varies between makes of alternator, but the difference between a modified and standard Bosch regulator is shown on p. 98 (middle right). Once the alternator is refitted, the wiring loom is then connected following the supplied wiring diagram, which also differs between alternators.

The small black-sheathed ambient-temperature compensation sensor is mounted within the section of wiring loom that runs to the batteries, so while making the battery connections the sensor can be located to a convenient spot near the batteries. As this measures ambient temperature it can be placed anywhere convenient within the battery compartment. Once all the connections are made the final job is to plug the loom connector into the Adverc unit.

An immediate improvement in charging and battery performance will be seen, but it must be remembered that even a sophisticated regulator cannot make an undersized alternator produce more than its maximum power, and although it will vastly improve matters, a low-powered alternator running at maximum output inevitably suffers.

UPGRADING THE ALTERNATOR

The accepted ratio between alternator output and battery capacity is 3:1 when using specialized regulators. Therefore a battery bank of 600 amp hours (fairly average) ideally requires a 200 amp alternator (or

A 130amp high output alternator alongside a standard vehicle unit.

The original alternator fits snugly on the engine.

The new, high output unit extends further away from the engine.

twin 100 amps). For practical purposes where one or more batteries are used for engine starting and are always well charged, this can be reduced. In many instances this ideal ratio cannot be achieved and this results in extended charging time. The problem with big output alternators is their physical size, which is one reason why engine manufacturers fit small alternators. However, in recent years small case alternators up to about 100 amps capacity have become available, and where this is considered a sufficient increase in power, will usually fit within the space of the original alternator.

A safety cover is fitted over the alternator main output terminal as it is close to the fuel filter.

The belt cover may need modifying to allow the new alternator to fit.

Fitting larger sized alternators is not always straightforward, but is worth the effort. As an example, fitting the Prestolite alternator to my Cummins meant swinging it further outboard than the original Bosch to clear the oil filter element and modifying the belt guard to suit. The original Bosch 70 amp alternator sits neatly within the engine hoses (normally protected by the engine belt guard). The new Prestolite 130 amp alternator needed the hoses adjusting slightly before it would fit.

Due to the extra length of the alternator body the main output terminal was very close to the engine oil filter element; should the alternator ever work loose this would cause a major short-circuit. To doubly ensure this could never happen I sheathed the terminal with a piece of rubber hose. This is just one example of the problems that can arise when modifying an engine, and another reason why it is more convenient for engine manufacturers to fit undersized alternators! Finally the engine belt guard had to be trimmed to allow it to protect the new alternator. However, the final job looks as neat as the original, and the charging performance is quite phenomenal compared with the original set-up.

Specialist marine electronics companies are able to advise on battery/alternator matching. Motor vehicle alternators perform perfectly adequately in a boat if protected from water and given an occasional spray with WD40 to prevent corrosion, and with cars becoming more sophisticated, large capacity vehicle alternators have become readily available at reasonable prices, whether new, reconditioned or second-hand from the local breakers' yard. In fact the most economical method of obtaining a good spare alternator is to buy one second-hand at the breakers' and then use it as an exchange for a reconditioned unit, rather than paying the surcharge for

The difference in size between a Bosch 70 amp and a Prestolite 130 amp alternator is quite considerable and may be enough to cause minor installation problems. Despite this the Prestolite 130 amp alternator is a good compromise between power and size, with the added advantage that it is designed to provide high output at low revs – on my own boat up to 70 amps at tickover, and this is a real boon to owners based on rivers. Alternators are generally designed to run fast to ensure adequate cooling. Slow-running alternators producing high currents can overheat unless, like this one, they are designed for the purpose.

buying a reconditioned unit outright with no exchange.

Two further points should be borne in mind if you are considering fitting a larger alternator. First, alternators for retro-fitting are not generally supplied with pulleys due to the variety of belt types and sizes, so refer to the engine manufacturer for a matching pulley. Second, you will need to check whether your chosen alternator requires a modified internal regulator. Many types only need a simple internal modification to the alternator that can be done either by the owner following the clear Adverc instructions, or by Adverc themselves at a nominal extra charge.

BATTERY ISOLATING SWITCHES

Cut-out switches to completely isolate the batteries from the electrical system should be heavy enough to carry all the current demands for the craft, including starting current. The main battery isolating switch ensures that the electrical system is dead when the boat is left unattended for any length of time. Apart from the safety

A one-two-both switch for selecting the domestic batteries is mounted in the electrical locker in the wheel-house.

implications, having the electrical system off ensures there is no opportunity for electrolytic corrosion from stray currents that would eat away at the stern gear.

Models are available to fit directly on to the battery terminal posts or for remote mounting. The latter type can be obtained in models for switching in two batteries, either separately or in parallel pairs. The drawback with this type is that longer battery leads are required, travelling from battery to master switch and then to the starter motor via the solenoid. Over very long runs this can lead to voltage drop causing starting problems, especially in very cold weather when the engine oil is particularly viscous, so care is required in the sighting of cut-out switches to keep cable runs to the minimum.

Remote Switching

Remotely switchable isolating switches solve the problem of long cable runs, as the main current carrying switch can be mounted near the batteries while the operating switch is mounted in any convenient position within the boat. Once remotely operated isolation switches are fitted there is no need to go anywhere near the batteries

A heavy-duty, engine start battery isolating switch mounted close to the batteries in the engine compartment.

when switching on or off, which means there is less chance of forgetting to switch off when leaving the boat.

In the example installation a pair of ETA remote battery isolating switches were fitted as direct replacements for the original Lucas battery terminal mounted switches. The work is within the scope of the average DIY owner and does not involve any special tools or skills other than those normally found on board a well equipped cruising boat. This installation was on a sea-going cruiser, so the work involved on a smaller boat may be somewhat simpler.

Pictured is one of the ETA remote isolation switches. The actuating solenoid is on top, with a thermal overload reset strapped to the side. This cuts off the *operating* current (not the main battery current) if the operating switch is held on for more than one second to prevent damage to the solenoid.

The photograph opposite above shows the complete kit prior to fitting. Note the two ply boxes designed to protect the switches once they are installed; fitted covers can usually be supplied if required.

To the left are the four operating switches; one on and one off for each isolating switch, plus the various cables required to complete the installation. The black multi-core cable is in fact trailer lighting cable, but its seven cores are sufficient to connect both switches in one neat cable run.

Fitting the Isolation Switches
See the photos opposite below and on pp. 106–107. The first job is to disconnect the batteries and remove the original manually operated isolating switches. Once a suitable position for the new switches has been decided upon, they can be fitted into place, in this case simply screwed to the board next to the battery compartment. With the new switches fitted, some of the original heavy-duty cables were found to be just too short to reach the terminals. Rather than replace the entire run, short extensions were made up with soldered eye connectors on each end; recently, heavy-duty crimp connectors have become the norm. When both ends were completed the new extensions were bolted to the original cable ends to make a reliable joint. To finish the

A remotely operated engine battery isolating switch.

A complete remote isolating switch with two home-made switch covers.

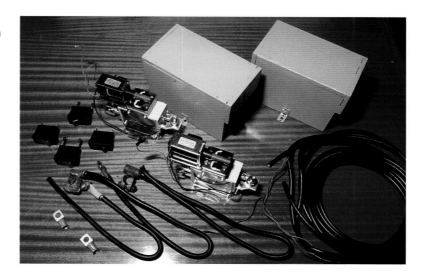

joints they were covered with both heat shrink insulation and insulating tape. The heavy-duty connections were then made to the switches themselves; these included the extended cables from the engines, and new short lengths of cable from the battery terminals to the switches.

Moving out of the engine compartment a position was chosen for the operating switches. This position had to be convenient, but not so much so that the switches could be accidentally operated when under way, cutting off the batteries. The chosen spot was to the right of the helm adjacent to the wheel. The position for each switch was marked, and after drilling a line of pilot holes a pad saw was used to roughly cut out the apertures; these were finished with a file.

The wiring for these operating switches is simple but a little unusual, as the switches operate on the negative (earth) side of the circuit. The reason for this is obvious. There is already a positive connection to the switch from the heavy-duty battery cable, but of course no negative connection.

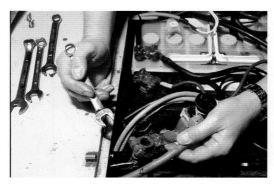

1. Removing the old on-battery isolating switches.

2. Mounting the remote switches near to the batteries.

3. Making up heavy-duty soldered terminals for the cables.

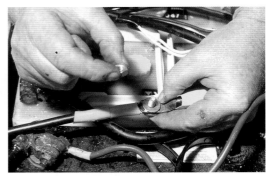

4. Joining two cables using the heavy-duty terminals. (New cables in one run would be better!)

5. The cable joint protected with self-amalgamating tape and insulating tape.

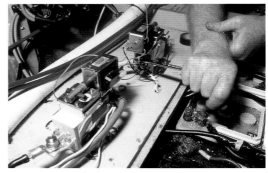

6. Making the connections to the remote switches.

7. Preparing the site for the operating switches near the helm.

8. A neat safety cover to prevent inadvertent operation of the switches.

9. Green for on and red for off: a simple and effective operating method.

Placing the operating switches on the negative side avoids the need for additional positive feeds, which would have to bypass the main switch and be permanently live to allow the operating switches to work. This is a very simple and safe solution.

To ensure the switches could never be accidentally operated a simple cover was fabricated to protect them. As can be seen, the switches are colour coded green for 'on' and red for 'off'. Even with the safety cover in place operation is simple, only requiring a momentary press of the spring-loaded switch to operate the main switch either 'on' or 'off'.

SPLIT CHARGING

If the engine relies solely on battery power for starting (as all large capacity marine diesels in common use do) then the two battery system – one for engine starting and one (or more) for domestic use – is essential and is not difficult to arrange.

Split charging has been around for some time and is the norm for electrical systems on most boats today, but with at least half-a-dozen possible methods of split charging available it can be difficult to decide which system to use. Split-charging systems vary in cost and sophistication, and in some cases also depend on the type of charging system installed on the boat.

For those less conversant with the workings of boat electrics, split charging is a method of charging both the engine start battery and domestic battery at the same time, but preventing both being discharged when the engine is stopped and the domestic electrics are being used. While the very smallest of boats manage without split charging, any vessel with pretensions to comfort needs a proper system to ensure the engine will start the following morning when away from shore power.

One of the myths of most split-charge systems is that the engine start battery is 'prioritized' within the system so that it receives the initial charge before the auxiliary battery begins charging. However, this would be a pointless exercise even if it worked, because the engine start battery is almost always fully charged having only to start the engine when required, and is the least used battery on board. This 'priority' system is based on charge voltage levels, so the engine battery is charged alone until the voltage rises to a pre-set level, where the relay cuts in and connects both batteries for charging. In practice using modern alternators the voltage level rises to the cut-in limit almost immediately, so in reality there is no 'prioritization'.

Manual Switching

The simplest and cheapest method of split charging is to use manual switching, with a single isolating switch. It is easy to install and works perfectly as long as the skipper remembers to switch off the connection between the batteries at the end of the

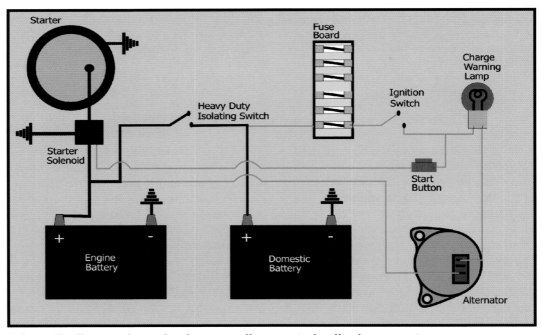

Schematic diagram for a simple, manually operated split-charge system.

A typical isolating switch used for manual split charging.

day's cruising when the engine is stopped. Failure to do this means that both the domestic and the engine battery are discharged together while lighting and other domestic equipment is being used. They must also remember to switch the connection on again when the engine is started, otherwise the domestic battery will not be charged during the day's cruising.

This system can be set up using a standard heavy-duty isolating switch between the engine battery and the domestic battery with the charge connections entering the engine battery. Alternatively a 'one-two-both' switch can be used, where either battery can perform as a domestic or engine battery, and charging priority can be given to individual battery banks, if necessary.

Simple Relay Operation via the Ignition Switch

See the photograph overleaf below. Not often used these days, this is the simplest of the automated systems but not the most reliable, as the relay is energized and connection made as soon as the ignition is switched on. In the event that the domestic battery is very low it is quite possible for it to draw down the fully charged engine battery before the engine can be started. A much better system using the simple relay involves a pressure switch mounted in parallel with the engine oil pressure switch, so that once the engine is running, the switch energizes the relay to allow the batteries to be connected for charging, or the relay can be energized from the alternator.

Voltage Sensitive Relay

The voltage sensitive relay (VSR) is a much better system; although it still uses a relay, in this case the relay is only energized once the engine is running and the charge voltage has reached a pre-set level. However, these systems can suffer from problems where high current is drawn from the auxiliary battery soon after start-up. If the battery voltage is drawn down to a level where the relay cuts out, then the auxiliary battery won't charge. In cases where this situation is critical it can lead to the relay chattering as it cuts in and out,

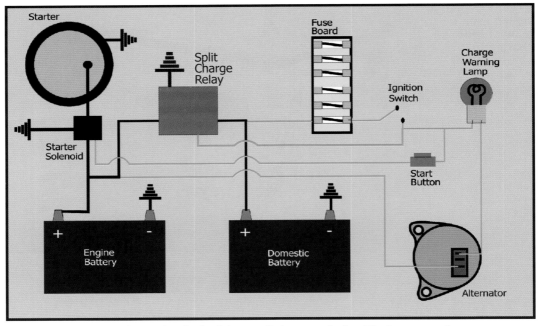

Schematic diagram for a simple ignition switch-operated split-charge system.

A heavy-duty vehicle relay will do the job at a reasonable price.

which causes arcing within the relay and subsequent failure. VSRs are not recommended for situations involving high electrical loads, small alternators and engines constantly at idle or low rpm.

Heavy-Duty Solenoid

This system is a more intelligent version of the voltage sensitive relay, operating in a similar but more sophisticated manner. It senses charge voltage in both the engine and auxiliary batteries, and once the required level is reached it connects the battery banks to allow charging of all batteries. In a high discharge situation where the battery bank is likely to be drawn down, this system will cut the connection between the batteries to preserve the charge in the engine battery. However, to prevent the arcing problems associated

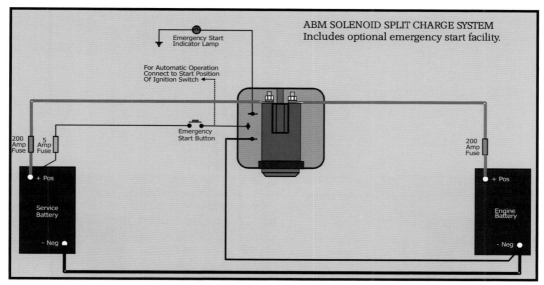

ABM SOLENOID SPLIT CHARGE SYSTEM
Includes optional emergency start facility.

Emergency Start
Indicator Lamp

For Automatic Operation
Connect to Start Position
Of Ignition Switch

Emergency
Start Button

200
Amp
Fuse

5
Amp
Fuse

+ Pos

Service
Battery

- Neg

200
Amp
Fuse

+ Pos

Engine
Battery

- Neg

Schematic diagram for an automatic solenoid operating system that senses battery voltage before making the connection.

with voltage sensitive relays the solenoid system incorporates a delay to prevent disconnection due to momentary fluctuations of charge voltage.

The compact solenoid that does the job.

DC-DC Charging between Batteries

This system is unique in that instead of the auxiliary battery taking its charge from the alternator, as in normal systems, it is actually charged directly from the main battery when the battery voltage reaches a set level. This system has all the attributes of a normal mains charger (bulk – absorption – float) to keep the 'recipient' battery in top condition. They are self-contained units with built-in fuse protection and are straightforward to install, and can be connected in parallel for greater capacity if required. Normally, charging only takes place when the engine is running, protecting the 'donor' battery.

Blocking Diodes and External Charge Regulator

This is the ultimate system for battery charging and split-charge systems. Blocking diodes offer simple installation and total isolation between batteries: whichever

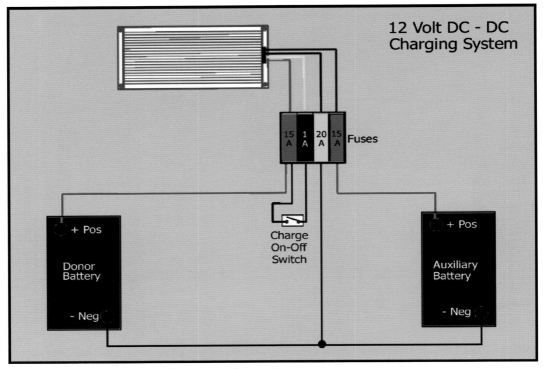

Schematic diagram for a DC-DC charging system.

The simple-to-install DC-DC charging module.

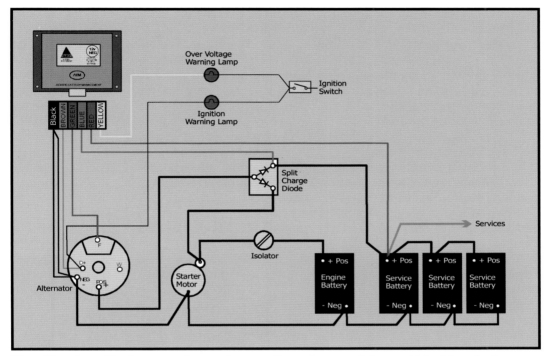

The ultimate split-charge system using an alternator regulator and blocking diodes.

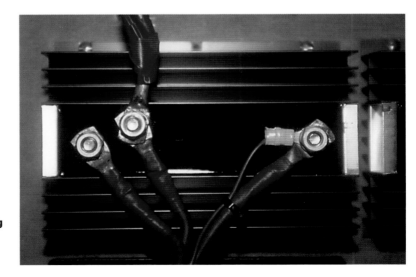

A standard 'SurePower' blocking diode with heavy-duty heat sink for cooling purposes.

battery requires the most charge automatically receives it, which means that every battery in the system gets exactly what it needs until all are charged to capacity. The drawback with blocking diodes, as we have already seen, is the voltage drop through the diodes; however, this is easily overcome by fitting an external regulator.

No Loss Charge Splitters

This may be a developing market, using more sophisticated electronic techniques, involving mosfets instead of simple diodes. Not much is known about these in terms of performance and reliability, and they are more expensive.

Combinations

Blocking diodes and one-two-both switches combine the merits of each system and are complementary to each other in providing more versatility, especially with supplementary charging systems such as solar panels, wind and mains chargers. Once again, however, a means of compensating for the voltage drop across the blocking diode is necessary.

The chosen system depends to a large extent on how the boat is used. If regular access to shore power is available then the on-board battery charger will keep things humming nicely, but if you like to get away from the maddening crowds and anchor beyond the reach of the shore power cable, then a reliable and user-friendly split-charge system becomes of far more importance.

INSTRUMENTS

Engine instruments are vital for protecting the engines from damage, and are often the first indication that something is going wrong. They can vary greatly in price and quality, and cannot generally be bought second-hand as the head unit and sender need to be matched. Car accessory shops are a good source of lower priced instruments, but these will not be protected

A typical engine instrument layout monitoring all the important engine operating parameters.

against the marine environment; however, a regular spray with WD40 front and back will keep help them in good condition and ensure reliable performance and long life.

Tachometers for diesel engines also vary in price and drive type. The simplest is the cable-driven type, but these cannot be readily adapted for dual helm read-outs and they are seldom seen except on much older boats; they also require long cable runs, which makes them unsuitable for larger vessels. Perception head types are easier to fit, as many gearbox adaptor plates are drilled to take them. Four shallow holes are drilled concentrically opposite each other in the face of the flywheel through the tapped hole in the adaptor plate, and a magnetic sensor is screwed in, leaving a gap of around 1/32in clearance between the face of the sensor and the flywheel. The sensor senses the engine revolutions as the drilled holes pass its face. Being an electronic unit, more than one readout is available, making it suitable for twin helm positions.

The most common and popular type today receives its signals from the alternator via a tapping in the field windings. Nearly all modern alternators already have a 'W' terminal take-off for this purpose, but if not, any auto electrician will make the necessary solder connection for a small fee. This type is also suitable for dual helm applications.

CONNECTIONS

Good connections are essential to a reliable electrical system, and every joint without exception should be made with either a soldered or crimped terminal. It can be tempting to twist a couple of wires together and bind them with insulating tape and the item will no doubt work quite satisfactorily, but by using this method a potential failure point and fire hazard is installed. Insulating tape does not last long in a hot and oily atmosphere, and once it has dropped off, bare wires are left just waiting to short out

The 'W' connector for driving the tachometer on an alternator connector block.

and cause a fire, or simply corrode away and break the circuit.

Heavy starter cables must be of sufficient capacity and have properly fitted terminals if lively starter performance (and easy starting) is to be achieved. Clamp-type fittings are the current recommendation for reliable heavy-duty terminals. Taper-post terminals should be properly crimped to the cable using a heavy-duty crimp tool. Ford-type block terminals require a heavy 'eyelet' terminal, which is also crimped; this same type of 'eyelet' should be used for connecting to master switches and starter motors. Various sizes of 'eyelet' are available from motor and auto-electrical shops as well as specialist marine suppliers, and it is important to use the correct size for the job.

Nowadays there is such a wide variety of crimp terminal kits readily available that there is no excuse for making bad connections. At one time all connections would have been soldered, but a proper crimped connection is as reliable as a good soldered one, and is very much better than a bad one. Crimp terminal kits usually include a cutting/crimping tool and a selection of terminals, including bullet connectors

A completed termination.

(male and female for in-line connections), spade connectors (also male and female, generally for equipment connections but also for in-line), and 'eyelets' in various sizes, mainly for threaded equipment connections.

Each type of connector is available in three colour-coded sizes to suit different gauge cables: red for the smallest cable sizes, blue for medium sizes and yellow for larger cables. Crimping tools vary from cheap but perfectly adequate versions to heavy-duty ratchet models that release when the correct pressure is applied. The tool has three crimping sizes which are also colour-coded to ensure that the

Heavy-duty crimp tool for making up starter cable and other high current cable ends.

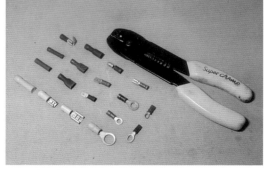

Standard crimp tool and a selection of terminals.

1. Cutting the outer sheath from the cable.

2. Removing the cable sheath without damaging the cable core.

3. A terminal of the correct size for the cable core is selected.

4. The cable is slipped in, and the terminal is securely crimped.

5. The crimp mark is clearly seen.

6. Give the cable a firm tug to ensure it is properly connected.

correct crimping pressure is applied to each connector. This makes it possible for the DIY enthusiast to make professional quality joints every time at minimal cost, with sets of connectors and the crimping tool costing as little as £5.

Making Secure Crimp Terminations

See the photos on p. 117. The cutting function of the crimping tool provides for various cable sizes and makes a clean cut through the insulation without damaging the copper strands. Once the cut is made the insulation can be slipped off the core using the tool. A terminal of the desired type and correct size for the cable is selected, slipped over the cable and pushed on until the insulation is felt to butt up inside. The correct colour-coded compression section of the tool is then placed over the terminal and squeezed as tight as possible to 'crimp' the terminal on to the cable. The finished joint will be neat and not at all distorted, but it is good practice to give the terminal a good hard tug to ensure it is properly crimped on to the cable. It should be almost impossible to pull off a properly crimped terminal; the only time I have known a crimp to fail is when a large terminal is used on undersized cable.

Other Connectors

Finally in the connection department there are the plastic connecting strips that have many uses as cable junctions and even in-line connectors; they are easy to use and infinitely preferable to the 'twist and insulate' joint mentioned earlier. This is a good item to have as part of the electrical spares kit, and will always make a reliable if bulky joint. They are particularly useful where several cables are to be joined in the same place. By placing the connecting strip inside a small plastic box the whole joint is protected and looks professional.

WIRING

All cables, whether for starting, charging or instrumentation, must be of a size heavy enough to carry the maximum load required, with a good safety margin to prevent overheating and possible insulation failure. The size of cable must be chosen with regard to both the current draw of the equipment and the length of the cable run: the longer the run, the heavier the cable must be. It is very important to note that the length of the cable run is both the positive and negative cable lengths – therefore

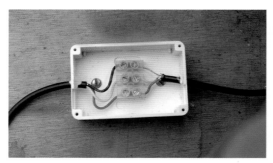

A connecting strip mounted in a box for security.

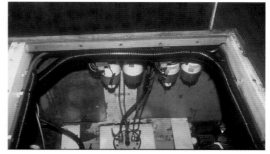

Flexible split trunking used to keep the engine compartment wiring neat and safe.

Spiral wrap used to manage the wiring behind an instrument panel.

if two-core cable is being run from the electrical panel to the equipment, the actual length of cable run will be doubled.

It is also important to bear in mind that the negative earth cable must be the same gauge as the positive cable. There was an idea circulating at one time that the negative cable could be much lighter, but if lighter cable is used there will first of all be a significant voltage drop, and it could also lead to the negative cable melting or catching fire.

Cable runs on the engine should be neatly loomed and protected using spiral wrap or split flexible trunking. Once away from the engine, cables can then be run in conduit to protect them from physical damage. An added advantage of conduit is that when extra circuits are required it is possible to feed additional wires through the conduit without disturbing the surrounding equipment and fittings.

Complex wiring such as that behind the instrument panel should be neatly laid out and can be conveniently loomed using plastic spiral wrap; this keeps the wiring neat, and allows plenty of air to circulate around the loom. It is good practice to avoid running cables through the bilges wherever possible.

Additional Circuits

Where dual battery systems are employed either with twin engines or a single engine and separate domestic battery, a useful addition is the facility to temporarily connect all batteries in parallel for engine starting should the main starting battery be discharged for any reason. This is simple to

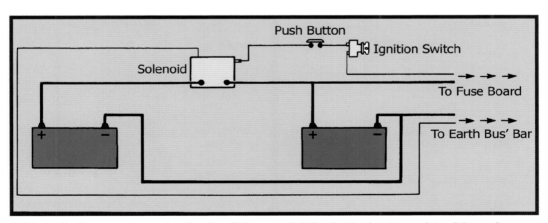

Schematic diagram for a simple circuit to parallel the batteries to assist with engine starting.

arrange by fitting remote starter solenoids between each battery, connected with heavy starter cable of the same gauge as the main starter cable. Solenoids are available from car accessory shops at reasonable cost, but it is essential to order one with the correct voltage of either 12 or 24 volts.

If there are just two batteries to be paralleled then only one solenoid is required. If three batteries are to be paralleled they will require two solenoids unless a selector switch is fitted between two of the batteries, which can select both and therefore

takes the place of one solenoid. The solenoid must be securely mounted near the batteries, and the body of the solenoid, if a vehicle type, must be earthed to the battery negative earth board, otherwise it will not operate.

The other connections are simple, with the two large terminals taking the heavy cables from each battery positive terminal, and the single small connector, which is usually of the spade type, taking the cable from the operating button. A press button is ideal for this purpose as it ensures that the batteries cannot inadvertently be left

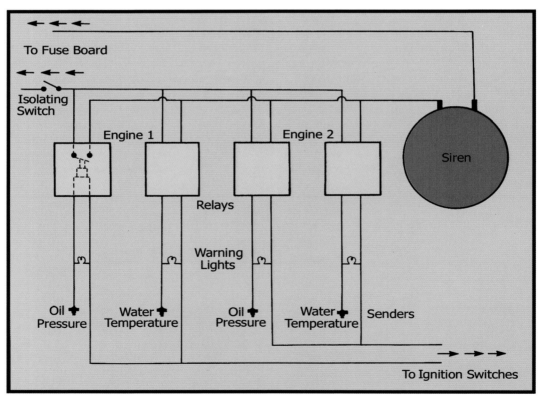

Schematic diagram for an engine-oil pressure and water temperature audible warning system.

connected in parallel, which would drastically shorten the solenoid life. A button designed for 12/24 volt DC use (also available from the car accessory shop) is essential for operating the solenoid due to the relatively high current draw when the solenoid throws in. The feed to the button is ideally taken from the ignition key switch so that it can only be used when the ignition is switched on.

Should the engine battery be too low to turn the engine fast enough to start, all that is required to operate the system is to hold the button in while turning the engine over, and to release it as soon as it starts. With all the ship's batteries in parallel this should result in the engine spinning fast enough to achieve a quick start.

Another useful DIY addition to the electrical system is an audible alarm monitor to warn of low engine-oil pressure or high water temperature (see the diagram opposite); this operates from the warning lights of each circuit, thereby utilizing the senders already fitted to the engine. This is particularly useful when an auto-pilot is extensively used and the instruments are not continually monitored, or when an inexperienced helmsman is on duty. It is also a good safeguard against unauthorized meddling with the controls when in harbour, as the siren will sound as soon as the ignition is switched on providing the isolating switch is in the 'on' position. In fact the only time the isolating switch should be 'off' is when the engines are first started so that the siren does not deafen everyone on board.

Parts required are accessory relays for each function, two relays for a single engine and four for twin engines, plus a high-pitched warning siren and an isolating switch. For engines without high temperature warning lights a low cost sender is available from Lancing Marine, which clamps to the water injection fitting on the exhaust manifold outlet and which gives early warning of raw water pump failure or a blocked water inlet strainer.

Clean and tighten the starter motor terminals, and make sure they are not swimming in the bilges!

The relays can be mounted in any convenient and dry location, preferably near the instrument panel and close to the siren. Wiring is straightforward, with a feed being supplied to the isolating switch from any convenient fused point. From the switch a connection is taken to one of the terminals on the function side of each relay. The connection from the other function terminals goes to the positive connection of the siren. The siren's negative connection goes to a convenient negative earthing point in the electrical system.

There are two connections to each warning light, and these are extended to the two operating terminals on each relay, with each light operating one relay. As soon as a light illuminates, the appropriate relay throws in and the siren operates. The total cost of this simple safety device is around £20, with all parts readily available from the local car accessory shop.

GENERAL MAINTENANCE

Older-type dynamos had an oiling point on their back bearing housing which required a few drops of oil during service, but later types and alternators are now generally maintenance-free, apart from an occasional clean and spray with WD40.

The starter motor is generally installed at the lower end of the engine near the bilge, and should be checked to ensure that it is not swimming in oily bilge water (*see* the photo on p. 121). It is worth disconnecting the main and auxiliary cables to the starter motor, and cleaning and greasing the contacts to prevent corrosion causing a high resistance in the joint, which will make starting more difficult and cause the terminals to become very hot. In addition, a good squirt of WD40 inside and out should keep it operating smoothly. (After using one of these sprays on any equipment, allow about fifteen minutes before operating, as the solvents in the spray are highly flammable and will be ignited by sparks in the motor.)

Check the bilges as part of the laying-up routine performed at the end of the season to ensure that water is not lying beneath the engine and keeping the starter motor and alternator permanently damp. This simple precaution should help see them through the worst of the winter weather.

CHAPTER 7

Turbochargers, Superchargers and After-Coolers

Turbocharging is a relatively easy method of increasing engine power by basically using a bolt-on accessory. The turbocharger provides forced induction, which simply means that combustion air is forced into the cylinders under pressure. This gives a worthwhile increase in power at moderate cost, making it the ideal method for manufacturers to offer the same basic engine in a variety of power outputs to suit differing applications.

The next step up the power-boosting ladder is to fit an after-cooler (or intercooler), which again often requires no further work than basic fitting and an increase in the fuel settings on the injection pump. After this it becomes necessary to rework the internals of the engine or to totally redesign the block – at which stage costs begin to escalate.

TURBOCHARGERS

To achieve diesel power-to-weight ratios approaching that of petrol engines, the use of turbocharging is now common practice.

'Turbo' has been the 'in' word with advertising executives for many years, though most have probably no idea of the meaning of the word. In fact it derives from 'turbine', which is the basis of the turbocharger. A turbine with vanes driven by the exhaust gases and rotating at 100,000rpm or more is connected to a vane-type air pump, which raises the pressure of the air entering the cylinders by amounts ranging from 9lb to 30lb, depending on the engine and its proposed use.

The increased pressure means that more air enters the cylinder, and this, coupled with a greater quantity of atomized fuel, provides extra effort to the piston on the downward part of the combustion stroke, resulting in more power from the engine. A turbocharger alone can increase the power of a standard engine by up to as much as 60 per cent depending on the pressure increase, but as pressure is increased the temperature of the air increases (think of your finger over the end of a bicycle pump) causing expansion, and therefore allowing a proportionately smaller amount of air to enter the cylinder.

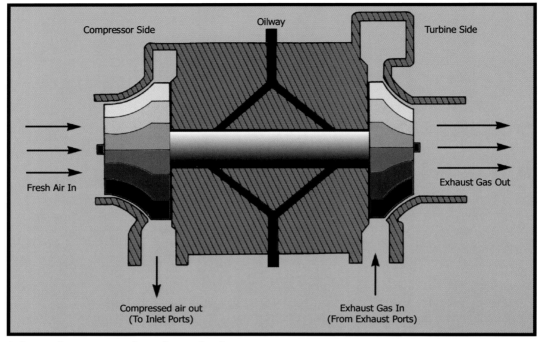

Schematic cross-section of a turbocharger.

A Volvo Penta turbocharger. The exhaust-driven turbine is on the right.

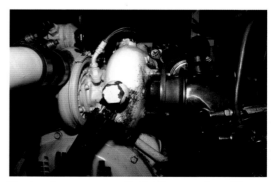

Turbocharger on a Cummins engine. The hot exhaust side is easy to spot!

As temperature increases a stage is eventually reached where the turbocharger is defeating its own object, as the air is so hot that it has expanded to the point where there is no increase in volume entering the cylinder.

AFTER-COOLERS

At this stage a charge air cooler is required if the power of the engine is to be further boosted. The charge air cooler, or after-cooler or intercooler, cools the compressed air before it enters the cylinder, which causes the air to contract, thereby allowing a greater amount of air to enter the cylinder. The extra air, coupled with a greater amount of atomized fuel, gives the extra power output from the engine.

The charge air cooler is similar in design to the normal heat exchanger used for engine water cooling, with a tube stack around which the charge air flows in a very similar manner to a car radiator. The cooling water passes through the tubes, but instead of the air cooling the water in a car radiator, the water cools the air. To provide the most effective level of cooling, raw water is usually passed through the after-cooler immediately after leaving the water pump while it is still cold, and in this way significantly reduces the temperature of the induction air.

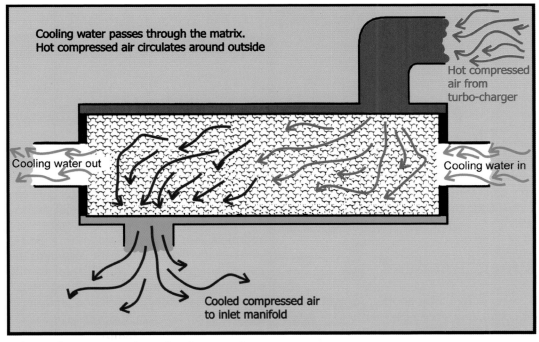

Schematic cross-section of an intercooler.

Raw water intercooler on a Cummins engine.

The tube stack (inset) is similar to a car radiator.

Thanks to the increased air flow into the cylinder, turbocharged and after-cooled engines are inherently more efficient, economical and clean running than their naturally aspirated counterparts. This has to be a very good thing in these days of high fuel prices.

SUPERCHARGERS

Superchargers offer another form of forced induction, and were a popular form of power boosting in the 1930s. Vintage car enthusiasts will be well acquainted with the 4-litre 'blower' Bentleys that had a large supercharger mounted in front of the radiator on the front bumper. The drawback with a supercharger compared with turbochargers is that they are mechanically driven by either a belt or chain, and as such draw large amounts of power from the engine to drive them. As speed increases, the power required increases and the benefit lessens. With modern engine design more power can usefully be extracted from the engine using good combustion chamber design coupled with turbocharging and after-cooling.

The problem with turbochargers is that they require plenty of engine revs to get them spinning up to speeds where the boost pressure increases sufficiently to give the required power increase. For most marine purposes this is not a problem, apart from sports cruisers that require a lot of power at relatively low revs to get them on to plane. Volvo were one of the first to find that the simple solution to this problem was to revert to old technology and use a supercharger to give the increased pressure boost and power output to get heavy sports cruisers accelerating rapidly on to

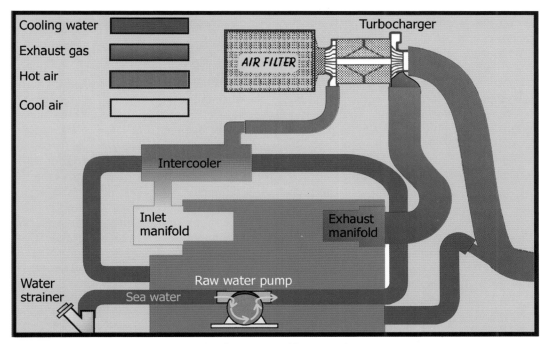

Cooling water

Exhaust gas

Hot air

Cool air

AIR FILTER

Turbocharger

Intercooler

Inlet manifold

Exhaust manifold

Water strainer

Raw water pump

Sea water

Schematic cross-section of a turbocharger and intercooler arrangement.

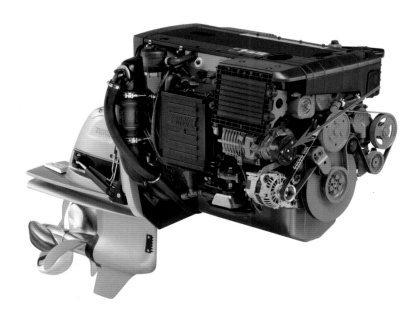

A 2009 300hp Volvo D4 with compact supercharger (arrowed), turbocharger and intercooler.

the plane. At a pre-set rev limit the supercharger is shut down by electronically disconnecting the drive-belt pulley and the turbocharger takes over, providing the best of both worlds.

Using a combination of supercharger, turbocharger, charge air cooler, modified pistons and common-rail fuel-injection equipment not only increases the power of an engine by over 100 per cent, but also provides much smoother running, now approaching that of petrol engines.

It must be borne in mind that the pressures on very high-powered engines are very high, which means greater wear and tear on the engine when used at full throttle. This makes it essential to match the extra power with enhanced servicing and engine care, with maintenance tasks carried out at shorter intervals. Engine oil and filter changes are particularly important, as the close tolerances of the turbocharger require clean oil at all times; this also means using the correct grade of oil, which will be of a higher grade than for unboosted engines.

For the express cruiser owner requiring ultimate power with diesel reliability, a diesel engine with forced induction is the obvious choice, giving the additional advantage of improved fuel economy power for power over naturally aspirated engines due to the extra fuel efficiency of forced induction units. Any engine, whether boosted or not, will reward its owner with long life and reliability if serviced at the correct intervals using high quality oils and regular filter changes. In fact, other than ensuring a clean supply of the correct grade of oil, there is no additional general maintenance work for the DIY owner to undertake on his turbocharger apart from removing it for service or repair if necessary. Due to the high revs and close tolerance engineering of turbo- and superchargers, repairs are best left to specialists.

CHAPTER 8

Marinization

Large engine manufacturers who also supply the marine market redesign and convert their own engines and sell them as marine units. This means the base engines are manufactured with subtle differences to make them more suitable for the marine field, together with the use of corrosion-resistant materials that would not normally be required for road or industrial use.

Specialist marine conversion companies such as Mermaid, who specialize in Ford, JCB and Steyr engines, and Perkins-Sabre who specialize in Perkins engines, must make such alterations as are necessary once they get the base engine into their workshops. This does not necessarily make one type of engine better than another, as both the original manufacturer and the marinizer take great care in the preparation of their finished product.

All engine manufacturers offering marine versions of their base units also supply vehicle engines, and each marine unit will have its counterpart in a vehicle. This means that spares from the local truck and van dealer will almost certainly be significantly cheaper than the 'marine' equivalent. A certain large engine manufacturer whose marine engine spares are legendary for their expense will deny that basic truck spares such as filters and belts are suitable for marine engines, but when the two types of part are compared they are generally found to be identical.

Many DIY boat-building enthusiasts will purchase second-hand engines from vehicle breakers' yards and after reconditioning, will convert them to marine use by buying similar parts to those used by the professional marinizing companies. This is a very cost-effective method of obtaining power for a boat, and at the end of the day all these engines are basically the same under the skin as their truck or van counterparts.

Converting an ex-vehicle engine for marine use is often regarded as a technical subject best left to experts and engineers, but for the do-it-yourself enthusiast with limited resources it is a very good way to save a lot of money when considering a replacement engine or when installing machinery in a new boat on a limited budget. The true marine engine, with its heavy build and very slow-revving performance designed exclusively for boat use, no longer exists for the average boat owner; instead, all the engines offered by the big names in the marine field are modified versions of light industrial car and truck units.

In many cases the only work required to turn a vehicle engine into a perfectly serviceable boat power unit is the addition of the water-cooling equipment, although with the present demand for higher power outputs many companies also modify the basic engines internally to accommodate this need.

CHOOSING AN ENGINE

The first and most important step is to choose a suitable engine. It is at this stage that the required performance of the boat must be decided upon, as this will then give an indication of the size of engine and power output required to provide this speed. Many people who are disappointed with their vessel performance have in fact fitted an engine which does not have sufficient power for their cruising aspirations. There are fairly simple formulae that will give a good indication of the power required for a given speed, while companies such as Lancing Marine can give specific advice on this matter.

This is a very cost-effective method of obtaining power for a boat, and certainly for leisure and light commercial marine use any differences between the base van and the boat engine are insignificant. There is not a great difference in cost between marinizing engines of different sizes when the engine is purchased on the second-hand market, so it is worthwhile to err on the larger side if this is possible: the extra power does not have to be used, but is always there if required in an emergency. This also allows for some loss of power due to wear, and the engine will be under less stress if it is never run at full output. The cost of marinizing parts varies between engine make and model, so check this before deciding on any particular engine.

Also, before making the final selection of engine make and model it is essential to check with the marinizing equipment supplier that marinizing parts are readily available off the shelf for that particular engine. There is little point in doing the job to save money if the engine requires extensive modification, resulting in large bills for one-off engineering work just so that the marinizing parts can be made to fit.

Perkins engines are a particular example of this as there are so many types of each model produced, some being very expensive to marinize, requiring extensive modification and additional parts. Similarly, some of the latest common-rail diesels can give problems as the electronics required to run them are often not included when the engine is sold second-hand, and these modules can add considerably to the final cost. Again, Lancing Marine are a good source of advice on this point.

The cheapest method of obtaining a basic engine is to buy from a local vehicle breakers' yard – though of course there is always an element of risk when buying second-hand, so it is advisable to have some idea of how to pick a good engine before buying. It is quite possible to pick up a low mileage engine in good condition requiring nothing more than a repaint prior to marinizing, and these usually come from late model vehicles involved in accidents that have written off the body; although more expensive initially than a well-worn example, they can mean a worthwhile saving in preparation time.

A good commercial vehicle breakers' yard will be able to start up the chosen engine while it is standing on the ground, and some, like our local Transit breakers, often have engines still installed in the vehicle for testing before being removed. It is worthwhile explaining what the engine is to be used for and whether it is required for immediate use or for reconditioning; they will then be able to select a suitable unit of the make and model decided upon. A check of the exterior of the engine for broken or damaged parts can then be followed by a look inside the rocker cover. The condition of the oil on the surfaces of the rocker assembly will give a good indication of the engine's internal condition; thus on a diesel the oil should be jet black; if it is also very 'sludgy' this may indicate badly worn piston rings. If it is milky in colour this indicates water in the oil, and unless it has obviously entered while the engine has been standing in the open it will be advisable to reject the engine.

While the engine is running it is possible to get a further indication of its overall condition. If it bursts into life from cold without hesitation and runs smoothly without undue smoke from the exhaust or obvious knocks and rattles, especially on the overrun and when ticking over, then the indications are that it will be in fairly good condition. A burst of throttle to see how responsive the engine is will also indicate that the fuel pump governor is functioning properly. (Care is essential when doing this on a free-standing engine to ensure that the torque does not cause it to topple over!)

For those who do not have the knowledge to choose a suitable engine, nor knowledgeable friends to assist them, a good compromise is to buy a worn example of the engine required at a knockdown price, then exchange it for a reconditioned unit from one of the many specialists in the vehicle engine reconditioning field. Like this, you have an engine that carries a guarantee and is ready for marinizing at a fraction of the price of a new unit. If this course of action is chosen it is essential to ensure that the engine selected is suitable for reconditioning, and in particular has no broken parts, otherwise the reconditioner will not accept it in exchange.

CHOOSING DRIVE

Gearbox

There are many makes of gearbox to choose from, and all the modern types are either servo or hydraulically operated, meaning that lightweight, single lever controls can be used. This will probably be the most expensive item on the marinizing shopping list, so if a second-hand unit can be found, large savings will be made.

Different makes of gearbox require different oils, and it is essential to use the correct type and grade. PRM and twin disc boxes use normal engine oil, while Hurth and Borg Warner use automatic transmission fluid.

Mechanical gearboxes are not really worth considering as they suffer from wear, and replacement parts could end up costing the equivalent of a good hydraulic box. Adaptor plates and drive plates are available from marinizers to cover most engine and gearbox combinations, which simplifies the job as all they require is bolting on and accurate alignment.

Outdrive

Using an outdrive can mean a saving on stern gear and gearbox as it performs both functions. There are fewer adaptor parts required, and they are fairly easy to fit (after ensuring that the transom is strong enough to take the weight and thrust).

Hydraulic Drive

Hydraulic drive is useful in difficult installations where perhaps there is insufficient room inside the boat to install the engine and gearbox in the normal manner, or where an outdrive cannot be used. In the marinizing sequence described below a hydraulic drive is used in a compact catamaran where a single long sail drive leg is fitted centrally and so is impossible to align with the engine.

Whatever drive type is chosen, the basic engine marinizing remains the same.

PREPARATIONS FOR MARINIZING

Once the chosen engine that will give the power required is actually at the workplace, preparations for marinizing can begin. If it is a new or reconditioned unit it will be ready for painting, but if it is second-hand the first job required will be a complete clean-down. Using an old wood chisel or similar tool as a scraper, the excess grease and caked-on mud must be removed before washing down begins. A proprietary engine cleaner from any car accessory shop used in conjunction with a wire brush and scraper will do a good job in removing the residue of the thickest dirt

Set up the engine for starting, and if possible arrange a supply of cooling water.

and grease. Once all the surface muck is in soluble form, a spray with a hose or, better still, a pressure washer will wash everything off.

Set up the engine for starting and if possible arrange a supply of cooling water to allow the engine to run for a longer period than was possible at the breakers' yard. A gravity feed to the fuel pump will suffice for the fuel feed and a mechanical oil pressure gauge screwed directly into the sender orifice will check the oil pressure (it is usually not possible to test this while at the breakers' as most modern vehicles use oil pressure warning lights rather than gauges). Run the engine and check that the oil pressure is within the limits stated in the engine manual. If everything still appears to be in good order stop the engine and allow it to cool down for a while. Unwanted items of equipment such as the exhaust manifold and engine fan (also the air compressor or exhauster on larger truck engines) can then be removed and discarded.

Unless it is quite certain that the engine is a low mileage model in excellent condition, it is worth removing the sump to check the condition of the crankshaft and bearings as well as the cylinder bores. If

Remove all the redundant parts.

there are no obvious signs of any damage or excess wear a new set of big end and main bearings can be fitted while the sump is removed. If there are signs of damage or wear it is better to discard the engine at this stage and get a replacement.

Once the sump is refitted, any obvious oil leaks – which should have been noted before washing down – should be dealt with using new gaskets.

Marinizing Equipment

The equipment required to convert a standard vehicle engine for indirect (or freshwater) cooling generally consists of the following:

- heat exchanger
- water-cooled exhaust manifold
- raw water or seawater pump
- oil cooler
- marine gearbox plus drive plate and adaptor plates (or outdrive)
- engine mounting plates and feet
- various other options such as sump pumps and power take-offs for bilge pumping and generators

Depending on the make of engine there may also be a need for other conversion items such as modified thermostat housings so that the new pipework will connect to the existing engine system.

It is quite possible to find all this marinizing equipment second-hand through boat jumbles or on Ebay, but this can lead to problems of incompatibility between different makes of parts, requiring extensive pipework for connecting up. Even so, although this will lead to an untidy-looking engine, it can be a big money saver that works perfectly well. If the complete marinizing kit is bought from a company such as Lancing Marine, it can be supplied with everything required including pipework,

which does make for a neater job, although of course costs are greater. Borrowing or hiring a tube bender can be a much cheaper alternative, and allows neat copper pipework runs to be made up for minimal cost.

Fitting the Parts

Fitting all the parts is really a very straightforward procedure, requiring only the most basic of engineering skills for removing the old parts and fitting the new. A set of the appropriate engine gaskets for fitting the manifold and items such as the thermostat housing will be needed, but if oil leaks have already been dealt with, then a complete gasket set for the engine will already be available.

If a complete marinizing kit is being used, then all the necessary brackets should have been provided; if the equipment has been collected second-hand, then it will be necessary to make up supports for items such as oil coolers – however, these are generally quite simple, although it is necessary to plan the pipe runs so as to decide the layout of the equipment. As already mentioned, domestic copper pipe and solder fittings are cheap and readily available in many sizes, which makes it possible to complete a very neat pipework installation without too much flexible hose trailing round the engine.

A good supply of hose clips of varying sizes will be needed to ensure that all the pipe joints are properly made. Good quality stainless-steel types are best as they will not start rusting immediately the engine is installed in the boat. Cheap stainless-steel types have little strength and are a waste of money, and many are not 100 per cent stainless – if in doubt check with a magnet: if it sticks they are not marine grade!

Of particular importance is the hose chosen: if possible, always use vehicle-type hoses, although reinforced clear hose will do as a second choice. On the suction side of the raw water pump it is vital that the hose is reinforced so it doesn't collapse under suction and thereby cut off the water flow. Beware, however, the spiral wound plastic reinforced hose available from chandlers, because some of this type actually shrinks dramatically when heated, and the temperature of the engine water is more than enough to do this. Check a piece in a saucepan of water before fitting. Steel reinforced rubber hose is the best, and although expensive, makes connection and removal easier than with reinforced plastic hoses.

The amount of work required will depend on whether or not the engine is a cross-flow type with inlet manifold on the opposite side to the exhaust. Where the heat exchanger/manifold is opposite the inlet, all that is required is to remove the old manifold, clean off the mating face on the engine block, fit a new gasket (if a gasket is specified) and bolt on the new heat exchanger manifold, taking care to tighten the securing nuts evenly and to the torque specified in the engine manual.

If the inlet manifold is on the same side as the exhaust it may need to be replaced with a new marine type, as in many cases the old inlet manifold will not clear the new heat exchanger. On some smaller engines the inlet manifold can simply be removed, and turned upside down. Remember to fit a new gasket and then refit the manifold followed by the heat exchanger/manifold, again tightening the securing nuts evenly to the correct torque.

It is difficult to be specific, but in this case the job was completed for less than £2,000, where you might expect to pay between £400 and £800 for an engine, then the cost of the marinizing kit (£800) and the gearbox (£600 plus). Of course costs increase with the size of engine, as all the parts will be that much more expensive.

Providing all the parts needed are to hand, then it is perfectly possible to complete the conversion, as we did, within twenty man hours of fairly leisurely work.

The engine featured here is the common Ford 1.6 diesel, as might be found on the earlier Escorts and Fiestas. Later models have a 1.8-litre capacity engine, and either of these engines is a suitable candidate for conversion to a life afloat. For this conversion a hydraulic pump was being installed on to the engine for driving a hydraulic motor in a catamaran, but the work is more or less identical when fitting a gearbox. Minor marinizing differences will

Mask the engine for painting.

Spraying with a DIY spraygun can give a more professional finish.

be found when converting other makes of engine, but again, overall the job is always very similar.

The basic engine can now be painted. Smooth 'Hammerite' is an excellent engine paint and is available from car accessory shops in a range of colours to suit individual tastes, although light colours help to show up any subsequent oil leaks. Once painted, the engine is ready to accept the marinizing equipment. Mask off any items that

are not to be painted as necessary, and then prime and paint either with a brush or spray gun, whichever is preferred. Spraying with a DIY spray gun can give a more professional finish, but a mix of brushing and spraying is often needed to cover all the nooks and crannies.

A basic marinizing kit will comprise some or all of these: gearbox adapter housing, heat exchanger, engine mounting feet, gearbox drive plate, oil cooler, raw water pump, a selection of hoses, copper tube and stainless-steel hose clips.

Oil Coolers
See the photos on pp. 136–137. Oil coolers for the engine and gearbox are usually mounted on brackets in convenient locations on the engine block where they can be neatly incorporated into the pipework run. At one time it was common practice to have the coolant drawn through the oil coolers before passing through the water pump, but this can dramatically cut the pump performance as the length of pipework through which the pump must draw

A basic marinizing kit.

1. The old oil filter is removed, and a long adapter stud fitted in place of the standard short stud.

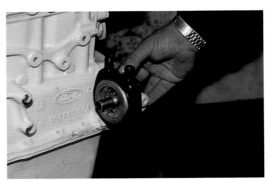

2. The oil cooler is fitted over the adapter stud.

3. The new oil filter is screwed tightly into position and secures the oil cooler.

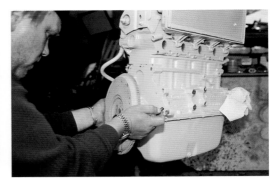

4. The flywheel can now be refitted.

5. Thread locking compound is applied to the threads.

6. The drive plate is bolted to the flywheel.

the water becomes excessive. The coolers should therefore be installed in positions where the water is pumped through them under pressure from the pump, rather than drawing the water through them. This type of compact cooler (*see* opposite) fits around the base of the oil filter mounting.

The old oil filter is removed and discarded, and a long adapter stud fitted in place of the standard short stud to allow the oil cooler to be installed. The new oil cooler is then fitted over the adapter stud and held in place by the new oil filter being screwed tightly into position by hand.

If the flywheel was removed for machining to accept the drive plate, as was the case here, it can now be refitted. Thread locking compound can be applied to the threads, and the securing bolts tightened to the correct torque as specified in the engine manual. The gearbox drive plate (or in this case, the hydraulic drive pump drive plate) can now be bolted to the flywheel.

Engine Feet and Mounts

Any engine installation on a pleasure boat will need to be on flexible mounts other- wise vibrations will cause great discomfort. The only type of boat able to use a solid installation is the very heavy steel or wooden working boat where the construction is solid enough to absorb vibrations. A modern, fairly lightweight craft will vibrate throughout if the engine is installed without flexible mounts.

When buying a complete marinizing kit it will often be possible to use the standard engine feet for mounting the engine, as the marinizer will have designed the package to suit these. In this case the marine feet come supplied as part of the marinizing package. However, when building a DIY one-off it may be necessary to design feet for the engine, but with simple welding skills (or knowing a friendly welder) fabrication is fairly easy. The flexible mounts chosen for mounting the engine will decide how successful the job of stopping vibration will be. It is best to consult an expert in this field such as Halyard or Lancing Marine for advice on the correct mountings to use for the size and type of engine.

The engine mounting feet are bolted into the block. It is important to ensure

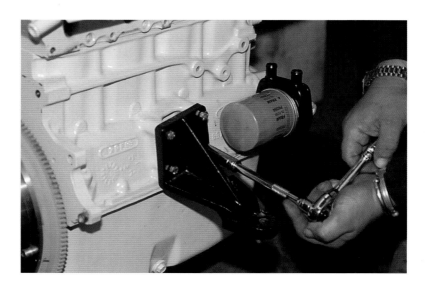

7. The engine mounting feet are bolted into place.

they are the right way round and on the correct sides of the engine; on some they will only fit in the correct place, but it is worth checking.

Heat Exchanger and Water-Cooled Exhaust Manifold

Manufacturers are increasingly turning to combined heat-exchanger manifolds as the main item of marinizing equipment as these are cheaper to produce than separate units, easier to fit and neater in appearance. Before installing the heat exchanger/manifold the gasket must be fitted. This is followed by the heat exchanger itself. The unit shown below comes from 'Polar' engi-

neering and is very fiddly to fit due to the position of the fixing studs.

A curved ring spanner had to be ground down to allow it to fit onto the nuts on the top of the manifold flanges. The exhaust water injection elbow is generally supplied as a separate part and this was fitted on to the manifold prior to painting the conversion equipment.

A new, more powerful alternator than the original had been purchased and painted black and was fitted on to the original mounting bracket. It is important when changing the alternator to ensure that the brackets will match the mounts on the engine. Another point is that the 'handing' of

1. The heat exchanger manifold gasket is positioned.

2. The heat exchanger is fitted.

3. A modified curved ring spanner to fit on to the nuts on the manifold flanges.

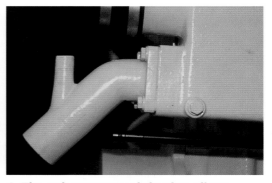

4. The exhaust water injection elbow.

5. A more powerful alternator was fitted.

the alternator; whether it was designed to fit on the left or right hand side of the engine is correct.

Raw Water Pump

This is a critical item if proper cooling is to be achieved and mounting will depend on the type of pump used. In Chapter 5 we looked in detail at the different types of pump available, with each having different methods of mounting and driving. Once the pump is satisfactorily mounted the main considerations are coupling the pipework so that the inlet rather than the outlet of the pump is actually connected to the boat's sea cock (an easy mistake to make) and that the pipework runs smoothly with the minimum of sharp bends and is well supported clear of areas where physical damage can take place.

A new internal engine water pump had been fitted as the original was suffering from bearing problems. The original water pump pulley was refitted along with the

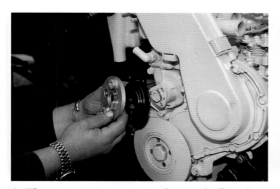

1. The raw water pump adapter is fitted.

2. The raw water pump is bolted on.

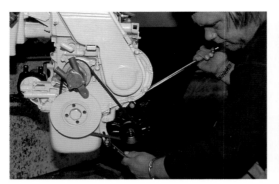

3. The alternator belt is fitted and tensioned.

1. The hydraulic drive bell-housing adapter plate is fitted.

adapter plate for the new raw water pump. This was followed by the raw water pump itself which is a high-speed type driven directly by the same belt as the engine water pump. The alternator belt was then fitted and the alternator levered outwards to bring the belt under tension.

Drive

Moving again to the back of the engine, the gearbox (or in this case the hydraulic drive) bell-housing adapter plate was fitted. At this stage the gearbox would normally be bolted to the bell housing, but as the hydraulic pump will power the drive motor, this was temporarily offered up instead.

The self-priming fuel filter assembly that had been removed for painting and a change of element was bolted back into place and the fuel piping reconnected.

Making up the water-cooling pipework

Now it was time to make up the pipework to connect the various marinizing parts together. Copper tubing of various sizes was used together with solder elbows to keep the amount of flexible piping to a minimum. As an example of one joint (*see* opposite), a tube cutter was used to cut the tube to length. (A hacksaw can be used but care is

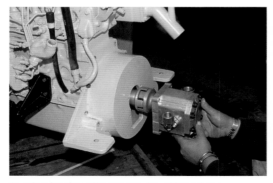

2. The hydraulic pump is offered up.

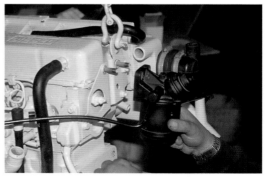

3. The self-priming fuel filter assembly is bolted back into place and the fuel piping reconnected.

1. Copper tubing is cut to length with a tube cutter.

2. Acid flux is applied to the tube.

3. The elbow is pushed on to the end of the tube and heated.

needed to ensure the end of the tube is cut square and all burrs are removed) Acid flux (from plumbers and DIY shops) was applied to the tube to clean the joint and help the solder run in properly. An elbow was pushed on to the end of the tube, and heat applied from a blowlamp while solder was applied to the joint. When hot enough, the solder runs into the joint assisted by the flux.

Piping Up

See the photos below right and on pp. 142–144. The water feed to the oil cooler comes from the vehicle heater take-off on the front of the engine. A short piece of flexible tube was ideal for this, and was secured with

hose clips at each end. The return from the oil cooler runs the length of the engine and was made up in 15mm copper tube and solder elbows, and connected to the cooler with a short length of rubber hose and hose clips. The alternative is to use a long length of hose, which is untidy and prone to damage. The engine end was then similarly connected.

The water return from the heat exchanger runs across the front of the engine and was made up in copper tube and elbows and again fitted using short lengths of hose and clips. The feed from the raw water pump to the heat exchanger was similarly secured.

The feed from the engine to the heat exchanger was simple enough to be run in

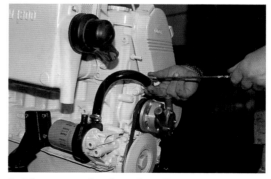

1. The water feed to the oil cooler is connected.

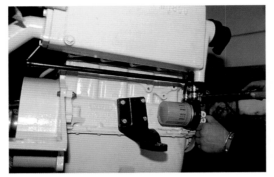

2. The return from the oil cooler is made up in 15mm copper tube and connected.

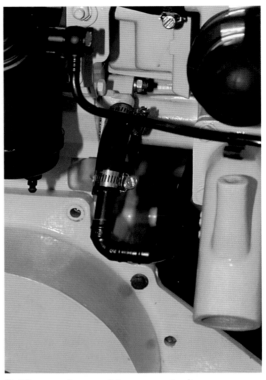

one length of hose, but the bend for the exhaust water injection inlet was made up in copper with another short length of hose to connect it to the injection elbow.

A plate is required to blank off the oil feed to the vehicle brake compressor take-off, and this was fitted prior to painting the engine and piped to the oil return in the block.

This engine has two air bleeds in the water system that prevent air locks causing overheating, and these return to the radiator in the vehicle and the heat exchanger in the marine version. The blanking plug must be removed from the front of the heat exchanger and replaced with a hose tail. The

3. The engine end is connected.

bleed pipework can then be connected between the three points. The original hoses from the vehicle have been used in this case.

4. The water return from the heat exchanger is made up in copper tube and elbows.

5. The feed from the raw water pump to the heat exchanger is connected using hoses and clips.

6. The feed from the engine to the heat exchanger is run in one length of hose.

The converted engine was lowered into its mounting cradle and bolted down on the flexible rubber engine mounts ready for

7. The bend for the exhaust water injection was made up in copper.

installing in the boat and coupling to the hydraulic drive motor. Finally the engine in its cradle was positioned and coupled to the hydraulic motor, and the additional

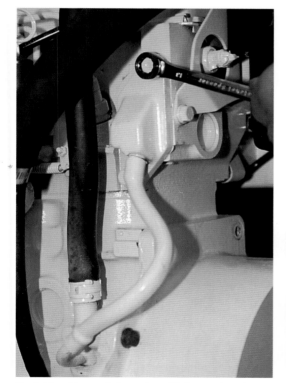

8. A blanking plate cuts off the redundant oil feed to the vehicle brake compressor take-off.

9. The air bleeds have their blanking plugs removed.

10. They are replaced with hose tails.

11. The bleed pipework is connected between three points.

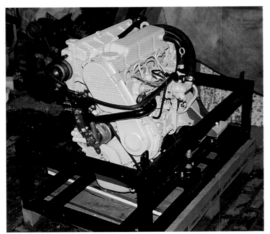

12. The converted engine is installed into its mounting cradle.

13. The finished job, with the engine installed, connected and ready to go.

hydraulic equipment such as the reversing valve and fluid reservoir were installed. Converting an engine for marine use isn't difficult, but it does need care if the finished product is to provide long and reliable service. Each make and type of engine has a slightly different set of marinizing requirements, but the Ford shown here is a good example of the type of work involved.

Shaft Couplings

When using a gearbox it is essential to allow a certain amount of flexibility between shaft and gearbox flange, and a flexible coupling will be needed. These vary greatly in price and type; probably the cheapest are the R and D Marine units, which work very well, while the most expensive will be the 'Aquadrive' from Halyard Marine, and Centaflex couplings from Centa Transmissions. These not only stop vibration being transmitted down the shaft, but also allow a degree of misalignment between engine and shaft which can make installation much simpler. They also incorporate a thrust bearing to take the thrust from the propeller via a heavy mounting flange bolted to the engine beds, rather than through the gearbox.

CHAPTER 9

Troubleshooting

There is nothing more disconcerting than the silence that falls over a motor cruiser when the engine suddenly stops while at sea. Good seamanship consists of being prepared for every occurrence, so carrying a comprehensive toolkit is the first step to getting the engine running again. The second step is knowing what to look for, and then how to rectify the problem when it is finally discovered.

Depending on the problem, it may be possible to restart the engine very quickly, but if serious trouble has occurred this may be impossible. The first step is to discover where the problem lies, and then to decide whether it can be put right or not. Apart from mechanical failure the problems that will stop a diesel engine can be roughly divided into three areas: fuel, water and air. While electrical failure can prevent a diesel engine from starting, it won't stop a running engine unless it is a very modern common-rail diesel.

Many engine problems can be rectified without detailed mechanical knowledge if they are approached in a logical manner, but a basic understanding of how each system works is of immense value when trouble-shooting. Troubleshooting itself is a matter of progressing logically through the systems until the problem is discovered. Most engine manuals contain a troubleshooting section covering basic and obvious problems that can occur with their particular engine. Unfortunately in my experience most faults occurring at sea are more obscure and are not included in the trouble-shooting guide. The old saying about 'a little knowledge being a dangerous thing' does not apply in this instance, as a little engine knowledge may mean the difference between wallowing in the swell or getting started and under way again in a matter of minutes.

THE FUEL SYSTEM

The most common diesel engine problems are fuel related and often begin with dirt in the fuel tank. Sediment in the bottom of the tank gets stirred up in rough weather and is then drawn through the fuel system where it clogs the filters and stops the fuel flow.

Indications of fuel blockage include erratic running and low power plus a sudden increase in revs before the engine stops. The first diagnostic step is to look (and smell) for signs of fuel leakage. A fractured fuel pipe will spill fuel into the bilge, even on the inlet side of the fuel lift pump. The answer is to repair the fracture and bleed the system.

The broken pipe will almost certainly be metal. Plastic pipes have no place in a fuel system due to the fire risk. An injector pipe should never fracture and any-way would not stop the engine except on

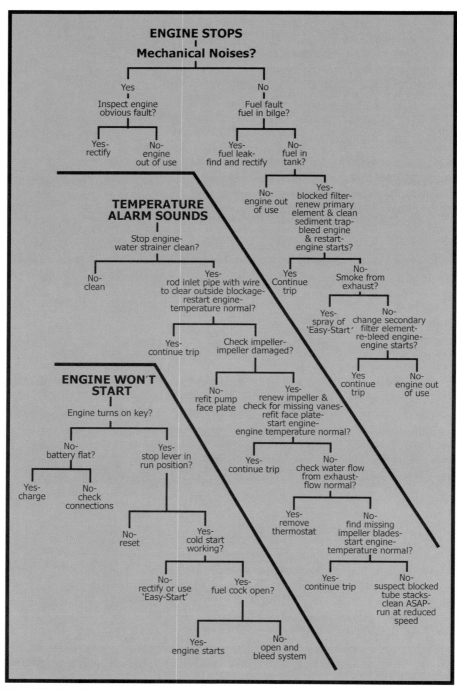

Troubleshooting graph.

A fractured fuel pipe.

Slip a piece of plastic hose over the ends and secure with hose clips.

single-cylinder engines, but simply cause rough running.

Fuel feed pipes can be renewed as a complete length by inserting a new section into the compression fittings at each end for a permanent repair, or by simply using a piece of plastic pipe pushed over the broken ends and secured with hose clips. A break on the suction (tank) side of the lift pump must be airtight or the system will not prime; on the pressure (engine) side some leakage will not affect the engine's running. Obviously this is only applicable to diesel engines, as petrol fuel systems must be tight and all spillages cleaned up before restarting.

With no sign of leakages and no harsh mechanical noises, but just the characteristic revving up before stopping, it is likely that you have either run out of fuel or the fuel filter is blocked. If you have run out perhaps you should consider taking up golf! Otherwise, fit a new primary filter and clean the water trap (if fitted). The secondary filter (if fitted) may be good enough to leave in place. To save time, do not change the filter 'O'-ring seals. *See* the photos below and on pp. 148–149.

1. Undo the filter element holding the bolt indicated.

2. Remove the filter element.

3. Save time by not changing the seals (if they are in good order).

4. Open the filter bleed screw to bleed the filter by manually pumping the lever on the lift pump.

Bleed the system and the engine should restart immediately; if it doesn't, change the secondary filter. Run it at reduced revs, as the problem may reoccur as more sediment passes through the system. You may have to reuse old filter elements to keep the engine running. Wash them by vigorously agitating in a bowl of fuel.

Bleeding the engine after a fuel stoppage will require bleeding of the filters, the fuel injection pump and the injector pipes, in that order. If the engine refuses to start, after bleeding check that smoke is issuing from the exhaust. If it isn't, then fuel is not being injected and the engine must be bled again.

If the engine does not begin firing almost immediately it is as well to conserve battery power by bleeding the system again before trying to restart.

5. Clean out the sediment trap – this is your first line of defence.

6. Find the location of the bleed screws on the injection pump (unless it is self-bleeding).

7. Slacken the nut on the injector to bleed the injector pipe.

8. Check the exhaust for smoke to ensure that fuel is being injected. Water will circulate with continual cranking of the engine.

THE COOLING SYSTEM

See the photo below and on pp. 150–152. Often the first sign of a problem is when the alarm sounds. The first step is to check the engine panel to establish what has triggered the alarm, as the low oil pressure alarm sounds the same. If it is safe to do so, stop the engine; if not, run on low revs to a safe area as there is no point in saving the engine if the whole boat is put at risk.

Possible causes of high engine temperature are a broken water-pump belt,

1. Slip a new fan belt over the alternator pulley when refitting.

2. A badly distorted impeller alongside a new one – one reason why they should be removed for winter storage.

3. Rodding down through the raw water strainer to clear an outside blockage.

4. Jabsco impeller removal tools for pumps of different size.

which may also be indicated by the charge warning light illuminating if the alternator is driven by the same belt. Fitting a new belt will solve the problem in a matter of minutes.

Water-pump impeller failure usually occurs at the start of the season if the impeller was not renewed. Changing the impeller will not in itself always solve the problem however, as the broken impeller blades are likely to be carried into the water system where they will partially block the heat exchanger or oil cooler tubes, whichever is the next piece of equipment up the line. After removing the remains of the old impeller from the pump body, count the number

5. Undo the cover screws or bolts.

6. Remove the cover plate taking care not to damage the gasket or 'O' ring.

7. Prise out the spindle cover (if fitted).

8. If you must lever out the impeller, take extreme care not to damage the edges of the pump body as this may prevent a proper seal when the cover is replaced, rendering the pump inoperable.

9. To use the impeller puller, slide the arms between the vanes and tighten the screws until they grip the impeller firmly.

10. Pull out the impeller by tightening the centre bolt.

11. Remove the impeller (and the key, if fitted).

12. Refit the key and install the new impeller by turning it to deflect the vanes while pushing it in until it engages with the key. Then push fully home.

13. Refit the gasket or 'O' ring and reinstal the cover plate, tightening the screws or bolts evenly.

of missing vanes. Fit the new impeller and start the engine. If the temperature returns to normal or near normal, make a note to dismantle the water system when back in port to retrieve the remaining broken impeller blades. If the engine remains dangerously hot the missing blades must be found immediately.

Water strainer blockage is unusual at sea, although large amounts of loose weed after a storm can cause a blockage. In rivers and estuaries there is more chance of picking up a plastic bag in the water inlet. If you have a Vetus-type water strainer with a clear top you can often see if water is circulating. If there is no water present and the strainer basket is clear, there may be a blockage around the outside of the inlet seacock. A rod pushed down the inlet pipe should clear this – the venerable wire coathanger is an ideal tool for this job as it will pass around slight bends on its way to the blockage.

Thermostat Failure

If the thermostat fails in the closed position, cooling water will be pumped around the engine but not into the heat exchanger for cooling, and this failure will quickly cause the engine to overheat. This will only happen after start-up, and the quick remedy is simply to remove it. The engine will run cooler than optimum, but will not suffer. Fit a new thermostat when next convenient.

Plastic bags or weed may block the water intake from the outside, but once the engine is turned off these may just drift away,

Remove the thermostat if the engine overheats after starting with a proper water flow through the system.

leaving no evidence of a problem. Restart the engine and if the temperature returns to normal assume this was the cause, but keep an eye on the temperature for the next hour or so. If the engine has over-heated badly and the temperature does not return to normal, check the pump impeller as this may have partially melted.

THE ELECTRICAL SYSTEM

Electrical system problems won't stop a running diesel engine (unless it is common-rail) but they can prevent it starting. The

most obvious problem is a flat battery, and unless the engine has a hand start or you have a generator on board, there is nothing to be done when trying to start at sea. Check the voltmeter reading and if it is below 10.5 volts or into the red sector, the battery for all useful purposes is flat.

If the boat has a split charge system with separate batteries for engine and domestic use and it is only the engine battery that is flat, the solution is either to connect the engine directly to the domestic battery or to use a set of jump leads to boost the engine start battery.

If the voltmeter is showing a healthy state of charge it may be a fuse or a bad connection causing the problem. Check the fuse board first, but if the fuse has blown there is likely to be another problem somewhere in the system. The bad connection could be a corroded eyelet terminal causing a massive resistance in the circuit. (The offending connection could be very hot, so care is needed when checking.) Dismantling all the connections, cleaning them, greasing with Vaseline and then reconnecting should solve the problem. On a split charge system the voltmeter may only read from one battery; if this is the domestic

Check the state of charge on the voltmeter. If it reads zero then either there is a broken connection or the battery is totally dead.

Use a multimeter across the positive and negative battery terminals to find the true state of charge.

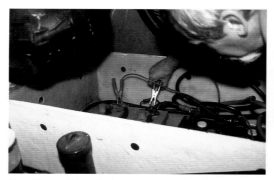

Use 'jump' leads to connect the domestic and engine battery to start the engine in an emergency.

Check the fuse board, and change fuses as necessary.

battery and it shows a full charge, the engine start battery may still be flat. Check the battery charge state directly on each battery with a digital multimeter; this will give the true state of charge irrespective of losses in the wiring loom and malfunctions in the voltmeter.

If the starter motor is clicking when the starter key is turned it may just be stuck through lack of use, and sometimes a sharp tap around the starter body will free it off. Also repeatedly turning the key on and off will often get it going. If this fails, removing the starter and freeing it off by turning the shaft until it turns freely should help.

Check the starter connections to ensure they are tight and not corroded.

Copious spraying with WD40 while freeing it off should help to keep it lubricated for future use. (Remember that the solvents in WD40 are flammable and should be allowed a few minutes to evaporate before trying the starter after refitting.)

If the problem appears to be in the low current feed from the key switch to the start solenoid, it is possible to operate the starter by taking a live wire direct from the positive battery terminal and touching it on the terminal from the key switch.

If the engine is turning over but not firing, check that the 'stop' lever on the engine is in the 'run' position; the stop cable may have broken or become disconnected. Also check that the cold start device is working. Heater plugs should feel hot to the touch after thirty seconds or so with the key in the heat position; if they remain cold use a little 'Easy Start' sprayed into the inlet to help start the engine.

PREVENTION TIPS

- Service the engine regularly. This dramatically reduces the risk of breakdown.
- If you are not confident about engine repairs, employ a marine engineer to

Clean out the fuel tank every three years to ensure a trouble-free fuel system.

rectify any problems as soon as they develop.

- Ask a mechanically knowledgeable friend to paint the important bits of the engine – the bleed screw, lift pump handle and so on – a different colour so you can identify them easily; use fluorescent paint so they can be seen in the dark, too.
- Keep two sets of spare filters, drive belts and impellers on board, so if you use one you won't have to go shopping that day for more spares.
- Go on an RYA diesel engine course – it's only one day and you will learn all the essentials.

- Put together a toolkit that covers all the essential repairs you may encounter at sea, including a proper impeller-removing tool from Jabsco.
- Keep a water-repellent and lubricating spray (such as WD40) on board, plus a can of 'Easy Start' engine-starting fluid (for emergencies only).
- Read the engine owner's handbook and learn the location of all the important sections that may require attention.
- Clean out the fuel tank once every three years.
- Make sure all fuel pipework is properly supported to avoid vibration fractures.

CHAPTER 10

Engine Installation

At some point it eventually becomes necessary to replace a boat's engine. If it is simply a matter of replacing like for like, then there are few problems to be overcome (apart from the cost!). However, if the engine is being changed to provide additional power, or an entirely different make of engine is being installed, then all sorts of problems can arise. The reason for the engine change will dictate the type and size of engine being installed, but assuming it is for more power then all the challenges associated with fitting a completely different engine will need to be overcome.

Before making any firm plans it is essential to ensure that the job is feasible both financially and physically – that is to say that the proposed new engine will actually fit! The first place to look is the engine bed and stern gear installation, because in some cases extensive modifications will be needed to the vessel to accommodate the new engine. Where this involves installing new stern gear and engine beds, the angle of these in relation to the waterline may affect the choice of gearbox or require the use of a universal joint coupling.

The choice of stern gear depends very much on the design of the vessel. High strength alloy shafts that allow smaller shaft diameters to accept greater power without twisting, although more expensive, can avoid serious additional work.

The added cost of one of these shafts over a standard 316 grade shaft is significantly less than the cost of converting the entire stern tube and shaft bracket to a larger size. The other great advantage is the corrosion resistance of the highest grades. 316 grade stainless steel is the standard grade for propeller shafts, while the lower 304 grade is occasionally used but is even less corrosion-resistant than 316 grade. Neither of these has the long-term corrosion resistance of high strength alloy shafts, so the extra expense is doubly worthwhile.

Having gone through the entire planning stage of calculating how much power can safely and usefully be installed, the engine and gearbox for the job can be selected. The next point is whether the original propeller shaft will be man enough to take the additional power, and if not, whether a high strength alloy shaft will do the job and avoid the necessity of cutting out and replacing the entire stern gear assembly. As already stated, replacing all the stern gear will add very significantly to the overall cost of the project.

In every step of the work it is important to check and recheck calculations; for example, when the engine installation drawings arrive, make certain that the close tolerances provided by the fully dimensioned engine drawing tally with the original rough calculations.

PLANNING CHECKLIST Item To Be Checked.		✓
Performance required. Maximum and cruising speed?	Max Cruise	
Is vessel's capable of providing the above performance?	Yes No	
Power required to achieve above performance?	Bhp kW	
Is vessel's hull capable of handling the above power?	Check with builder:	
Propeller shaft diameter is correct for the torque produced?	Check with Prop' supplier:	
Propeller shaft diameter required for the torque produced?	Inches mm	
Up-size the entire stern-gear to meet above requirements?	Yes No	
Specify high strength alloy shaft as alternative to above?	Yes No	
Warranties offered by different engine suppliers compared?	Yes No	
Suitable gearbox/es to handle the power of the engine/s selected. (See below also)	Make and Type:	
Gearboxes selected with capacity for engine's power?	Yes No	
Gearboxes can run continuously in either direction for contra-rotation in twin engine installations?	Yes No	
For twin engines, gearboxes selected with identical forward and reverse ratios?	Yes No	
Duty cycle for chosen engine is correct for vessel's proposed operation?	Duty cycle type:	
Room in the engine compartment to fit the engine/s?	Yes No	
Sufficient ventilation within the engine compartment for the engine's combustion and cooling needs?	Required Cross section of engine comp' vents	
Modifications required within the vessel are feasible?	Yes No	
Sufficient propeller tip clearance for larger propellers to suit new engine?	Required prop' diameter Tip clearance:	
Suitable location for performing the work?	Place:	
Lifting equipment available?	Yes No	

The basic pre-planning process.

PREPARATION

Most companies supply comprehensive installation manuals to ensure that any engineer can install the engine in the correct manner and to the manufacturer's recommendations. Once all the calculations have been verified to be correct, the old engine can be removed to allow the engine compartment to be prepared for the new unit.

If the boat has a hatch designed into the roof for engine removal (or the engine is mounted beneath the floor in an open cockpit), then lifting out will not be a problem. If the boat appears to have been built around the engine it may need to be dismantled in situ and removed in bits.

Even with a dedicated hatch, engines are often longer than the hatch opening, which will mean experimenting with the lifting angle until the engine can be hauled out of the engine compartment and through the hatch. Once the old engine is out of the boat, any items to be transferred to the new engine can now be removed, such as high-output alternators that are not normally supplied as standard.

The original propeller will need to be removed before sliding out the old propeller shaft. In most boats there is either a hole in the rudder or the rudder is offset slightly to allow the prop shaft to be removed without having to take off the rudder.

Lifting out the old engine nose up to allow it to pass through the roof hatch.

The old propeller ready for removal.

Removing the propeller shaft with the rudder also removed for easier access.

Occasionally it is easier to remove the rudder to simplify access to the shaft and stern tube.

Shaft bearings will need replacing before a new shaft is fitted, so these can be removed as soon as the shaft is out of the way. The grub screws securing the bearing must first be loosened and removed, after which the bearing can be pulled out. If the bearing has a phenolic composite laminate body it is easiest to break it up using a wood chisel prior to removal; it will then come out of its housing quite easily. If the bearing has a brass body it may be corroded in and will need a puller to remove it. Phenolic-bodied bearings are cheaper and do not suffer from this corroding problem, making them the ideal choice.

Drawings detailing the engine mounts in the boat and the mounting feet on the new engine can be produced to see whether the mounts need to be raised or lowered to allow the gearbox coupling to mate with the propeller shaft. It is also important to check that the mounting feet are the same width apart, because if they are not the difference

Undoing the grub screws securing the bearing in the tube.

Breaking up a phenolic-bodied bearing to ease removal.

Once collapsed the old bearing should come out easily.

will also need to be accommodated. If the difference in the mounting height and/or width is substantial, then the old engine beds will need to be modified.

Before altering the engine beds, carefully measure the position of the mounting feet in relation to the gearbox output flange. The new propeller shaft will need to be installed to provide the fore and aft position of the engine on the beds. If the engine beds are marked in line with the shaft coupling face, the final position of the engine mounting feet can be measured from these marks. The position of the engine mounting feet can be marked on to the beds, and that of the raised engine beds finalized.

On a GRP or wooden vessel the new beds would normally run the full length of the old beds and be either bolted or bonded into position. This saves the need to accurately measure the fore and aft position of the feet at this stage, as the engine position can be altered by sliding it fore and aft to suit the propeller shaft coupling once roughly in position. On steel vessels the beds can be raised locally, but this requires greater accuracy in the final fore and aft positioning of the engine.

Apart from altering the engine mounts, it is quite possible that items such as floor supports will need to be adjusted to make room for equipment mounted on the new engine. For timber or GRP vessels the cutting out of floor supports to make way for the engine is probably more straightforward than on a steel vessel, but it is important

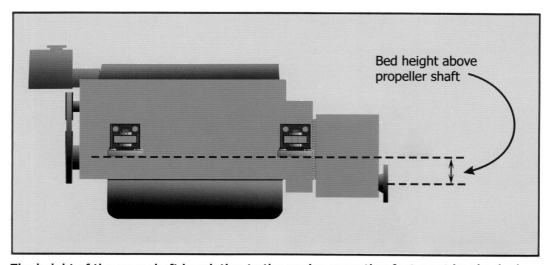

The height of the prop shaft in relation to the engine mounting feet must be checked.

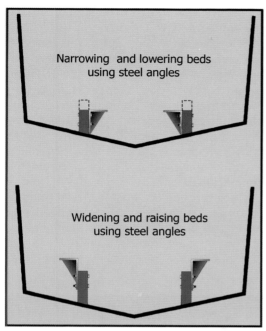

The width of the new engine feet must also be checked to see whether the mounts need alteration.

The new propeller shaft, coupling flange and propeller ready for installation.

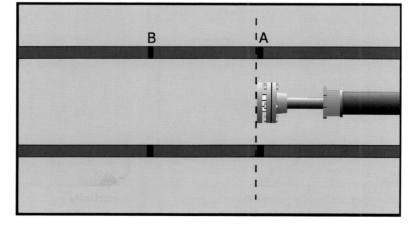

The position of the end of the prop shaft may decide the fore and aft position of the engine, so it needs to be checked.

The engine bed raised on a steel vessel to provide the correct propeller shaft alignment.

to ensure that the rebuilt supports have the same strength as the originals.

With the old engine out of the way and the engine compartment thoroughly degreased and freshly painted, the old flexible exhaust hoses and silencer can be removed and the new equipment, which will generally be larger, offered up. Any alterations required to allow the new exhaust to pass through the bulkheads can be made while there is plenty of room in the engine compartment.

Once through the bulkhead and into the accommodation, the exhaust runs need to be led to their outlets, which may require alterations to the accommodation. New exhaust outlets will almost certainly be required,

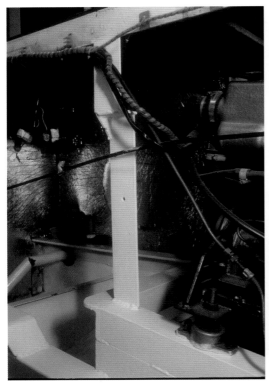

An adjusted wheelhouse floor support to make room for the new engine.

A partially rebuilt engine compartment still covered in 'muck'.

The same engine compartment cleaned and painted.

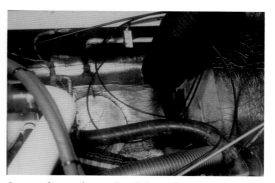

A new large bore flexible exhaust hose running along the top of the picture and through the engine compartment bulkhead.

The new custom-made exhaust transom fitting.

Adjusting a drawer unit to allow the large bore exhaust to run through the accommodation. The exhaust was later covered with carpet and was then unnoticeable.

Access hole cut into a panel to allow the exhaust hose to connect to the transom fitting.

like the custom-made unit illustrated opposite, to handle the exhaust from the new main engine and old original wing engine. Running the exhaust may also mean cutting various access hatches into the floor and other areas. However, with care even a large exhaust running through the accommodation can be disguised well enough not to be intrusive.

STERN GEAR AND ENGINE BEDS

Installing the Engine Beds and Propeller Shaft

In most cases of re-engining a total rebuild of the engine beds and stern gear will not be required. However, in some cases there may unfortunately be no other option than to make radical changes to the boat to enable a larger engine to be installed. The most likely reason for major changes is when there is insufficient space between the hull and propeller shaft to accommodate the radius of the required propeller. Where the problem is marginal the propeller manufacturer will often be able to redesign the propeller with a smaller diameter and compensate for this with greater blade

area and pitch. Where the change required is very large, the only solution is to lower the outboard end of the shaft by increasing the angle at which it passes through the hull. Unfortunately the difference between the old and new propeller sizes may make the increased shaft angle too great to allow the engine beds to be realigned. There may also be a problem with clearance beneath the cockpit floor that only the use of a down-angle gearbox will solve.

Every engine has a maximum installation angle that must not be exceeded due to the design of the oil pick-up in the sump. In this case the work may be greatly simplified by using a down-angle gearbox. This will almost certainly provide the additional angle required to accommodate the new shaft attitude without making significant alterations to the engine beds other than minor reshimming during final coupling alignment.

Designing the Engine Beds

There are various methods of designing engine beds to suit any particular engine. Drawings of the engine can be prepared, taking into account the relationship between the various installation components. The position of the gearbox output shaft provides the final position of the engine on

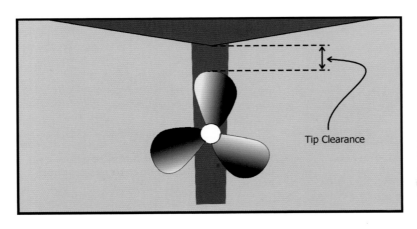

Tip Clearance

Sufficient propeller tip clearance is essential to prevent excess noise and water wear on the hull bottom.

The engine may need to be tilted to give the necessary tip clearance. However, cockpit floor clearance may also be a problem. Note the difference between dimension AB with a standard gearbox and CD with a down-angle gearbox.

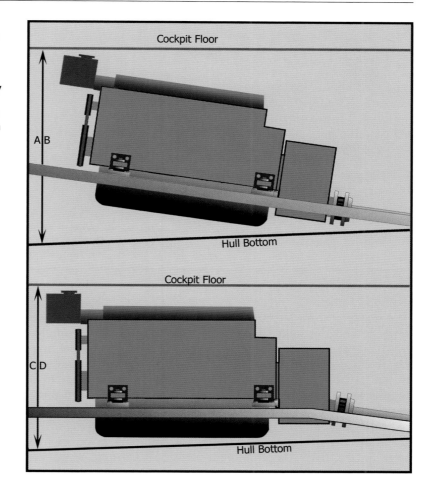

If the angle is too great for the engine, a down-angle gearbox may be the only solution.

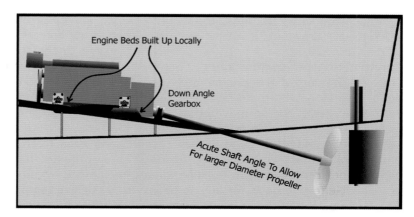

Allow for
sump clearance

Sump clearance must be checked to ensure there is room beneath the engine beds and the hull.

the beds in the fore and aft plane. The vertical distance between the rubber mounting feet bottoms and the propeller shaft line gives the height of the beds in relation to the propeller shaft. The depth of the lowest part of the sump below the mounting feet bottoms ensures that the engine is in fact far enough forward on the beds to clear the hull skin. Finally the width apart of the mounting feet provides the distance between the beds. Another method is to make up a simple ply mock-up of the engine incorporating all the above dimensions. This makes it easier to visualize the final installation for those less used to working with drawings.

Constructing the Engine Beds

The construction of the engine beds depends largely on the material of the hull. For a steel vessel the normal method is to weld in large steel angle irons and stiffen them with welded cross-members. For timber craft, massive baulks of second-hand timber retrieved from building sites are a cost-effective basis for engine beds. These can be cut to shape using a circular

saw after first removing old nails from the timber. With the correct angle ascertained from the string line it is short work cutting the timber to shape, after which the pieces can be bolted and glued into position. The same method is also used for GRP vessels, except in this case the beds are bonded into position. Additional cross-members can be added as necessary to suit the engine design and to add to the structural stiffness of the vessel's hull.

Constructing the Engine Mounting Frame

Once the basic engine beds are in place and at the correct angle, many people find it easier to construct an engine mounting frame away from the boat. The basic full strength engine beds must be installed within the boat to accept the weight of the engine and to transmit the thrust of the propeller, but they do not have to be constructed to the exacting requirements of the engine. Instead, the needs of the engine are accommodated by the frame, and this is often an easier option when re-powering than totally rebuilding the engine

An engine mounting frame will often make the entire job simpler.

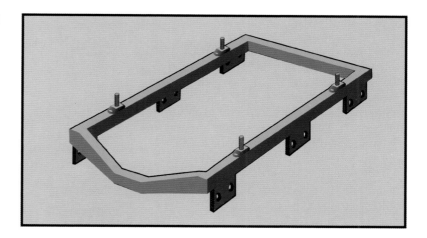

beds, depending on how different the old and new engines are. The frame is the secondary engine bed that will eventually be bolted or welded on to the primary engine bed built into the boat.

The frame in its most basic form consists of steel angle irons running each side of the engine, on to which the engine mounting feet will be bolted. It must be strong enough to support the weight of the engine and to accept the thrust of the propeller once installed; 4 x 4in (100 x 100mm) angle irons are strong enough for engines up to about 10-litre capacity. Cross-members welded between the two outer angles complete the frame, while webs and stiffeners are added as required.

During construction, allowance will be made for the sump and the gearbox output shaft so that when the frame is complete the engine sits on it without any parts fouling the frame. If the position of the gearbox output shaft is marked on the frame prior to its installation, it will act as a guide to the final position of the frame (and therefore the engine) once installed. As the frame is a fraction of the weight of the engine it can be positioned accurately on to the primary engine beds to allow the

fixing flanges to be made up and welded on to the frame prior to engine installation. This type of frame can usefully be used for all types of boat construction as the final fastening into place can be either by welding or by bolting.

Ventilation

When working with fibre-glass materials in the confined space of an engine compartment it is important to make proper preparations for ventilating the area before commencing fibre-glassing. Industrial extractor fans can be hired from the local plant hire shop, and are well worth the small cost involved. A plentiful supply of cheap plastic gloves to protect hands from the catalyzed resin is another essential.

Mounting the Couplings

Where a non-aligned shaft installation is required but a down-angle gearbox is not desired, possibly because the original gearbox is to be used for the new installation, then a universal joint coupling must be used. 'Aqua-Drive' and Centaflex couplings are popular due to their relative ease of installation and time-proven reliability.

As both these couplings incorporate a heavy-duty thrust bearing to accept the thrust of the propeller, it is important that they are strongly mounted. The usual method is to fabricate a steel cross-member that is either bolted or welded between the engine beds at the inboard end of the propeller shaft. This must be strong enough to transmit the thrust of the propeller to the boat without any movement or give.

Once the thrust-bearing carrier is installed it is then easy to couple the universal joint shaft to the gearbox output shaft. The only point to watch is that the two universal joints in the system are both at the same angle, and that in a non-aligned installation the angle between shaft and engine does not exceed the recommended maximum for the universal joint coupling.

INSTALLING THE NEW ENGINE

Placing the Engine on the Engine Beds

Once all the preparation is complete, the actual physical placing of the engine on to the new engine beds can begin. Safety is a major consideration when working in an

Lifting begins with the engine nose up to allow it to pass through the hatch.

All the parts that make the engine too wide to pass through the opening will need to be removed.

The tilted engine is passed gearbox first into the hatch, but is obstructed by a small bracket.

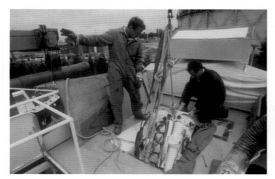

Once the bracket was removed, the engine passed easily through the hatch.

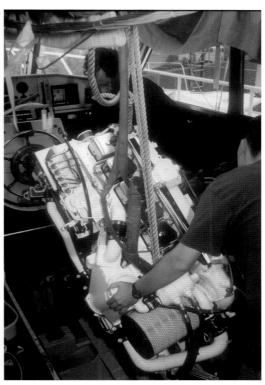

Once inside, the engine had to be chocked up and reslung so it could be lowered correctly on to the mounts.

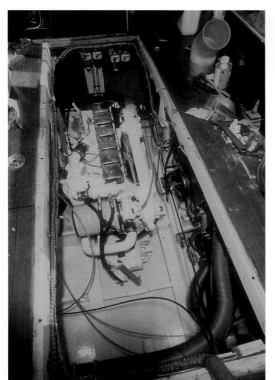

The engine finally sitting in position.

industrial environment. Whether the work is being performed in the garden at home or within the confines of a boatyard it is still very much an industrial project, with all the inherent risks involved. An engine weighing in at around a ton needs care when handling. It is not only the avoidance of injury that must be borne in mind, but also the cost of replacing anything that becomes damaged, and these are two very good reasons for using a crane for all lifting work on big engines. Most marinas have a crane of some sort for general lifting purposes and this, together with an experienced operator, makes the work very much easier.

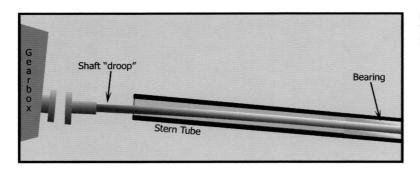

Check for shaft 'droop' on long shaft lengths.

Preparation for lifting may consist of removing various parts from the engine to allow it to pass through the available opening in the hatch. Items such as the heat exchanger, exhaust water injection elbow and the oil filter assembly are likely to need removal. When it is only isolated parts that are extending out further than the required width, the engine can usually be twisted and tilted around to avoid these parts while it is hanging in the slings – and if the old engine had to be tilted for lifting out, then it is fairly certain that the new, larger lump will require similar treatment.

Before beginning the lift it is worth arranging blankets all round the hatch opening to try and minimize damage to the engine or the hatch surround during lowering in. If all goes well the tilted engine will pass through the opening without further ado; however, more often than not something unexpected will foul the hatch and need further dismantling – even a small relay bracket bolted to the starter motor mounting is enough to delay matters. With all the obstructions cleared, the engine can continue its journey through the hatch and down into the engine compartment.

An engine in a nose-up attitude will almost certainly require reslinging and straightening up before it will sit properly in the prepared beds. To achieve this it will need chocking up at floor level to enable the slings to be refitted, thereby allowing the engine to hang level. It should then lower neatly into position and sit on the prepared beds.

The next step is to ensure there is no 'droop' in the shaft between the last bearing and the coupling end of the shaft. This is only necessary when the shaft is long and there is a large unsupported length of shaft between the last bearing and the coupling. To find whether droop is a factor, the spacing between the shaft and stern-

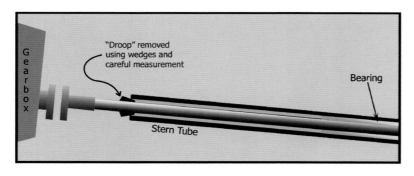

Remove any 'droop' by using wedges.

Typical engine rubber mount.

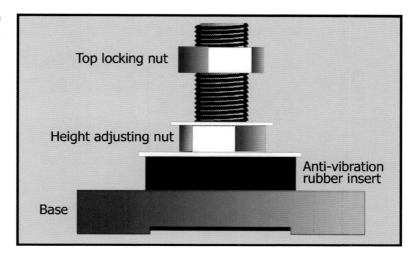

Top locking nut

Height adjusting nut

Anti-vibration rubber insert

Base

tube is measured top and bottom, left and right and the shaft supported with wedges until the 'droop' is removed.

Alignment of the Gearbox Coupling and the Propeller Shaft

The next job is to check the alignment of the gearbox coupling and the propeller shaft. This will not be perfect to start with, as there is a degree of adjustment pro-vided on the rubber engine mounting feet. However, it is important to keep the engine feet as low as possible in the mounts to avoid excessive forward motion on the rubbers when in gear and the propeller is applying thrust to the gearbox.

The position of the engine mounting fixing bolt holes decides the final athwartship position of the engine, and it is therefore vital to get the engine aligned with the

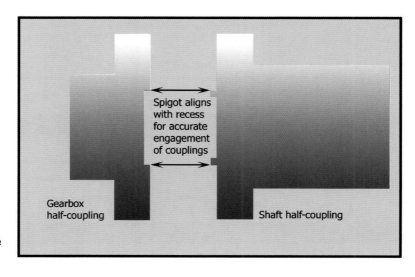

Spigot aligns with recess for accurate engagement of couplings

Gearbox half-coupling

Shaft half-coupling

Coupling face alignment.

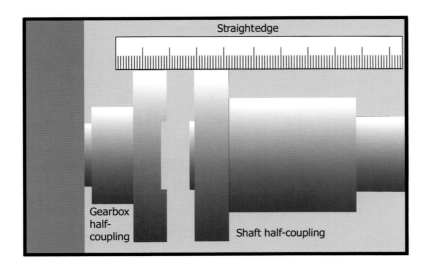

Using a straightedge to check linear alignment.

shaft coupling before drilling the holes. The flexible engine mounts have slotted holes to allow a small amount of athwartship movement for final alignment, but this is not sufficient for correcting large errors; it is therefore important to get the initial alignment as near perfect as possible.

Correcting Angular and Linear Misalignment

With a portable hoist set up on blocks at floor level to make moving the engine less arduous, initial engine and shaft alignment can begin. Roughly align the engine with the shaft by physically moving it across the beds to align the coupling faces. At this stage a lot of fiddling about can ensue as the engine is moved around to get the initial angular and linear alignment correct. Angular alignment refers to the mating of the coupling faces to ensure that when they are bolted together they are perfectly flush fitting. If there is any angular misalignment the shaft will run with a permanent twist, setting up vibration and stress on the shaft, bearings and gearbox, leading to

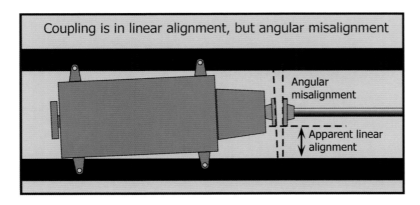

Checking angular misalignment.

Checking linear misalignment.

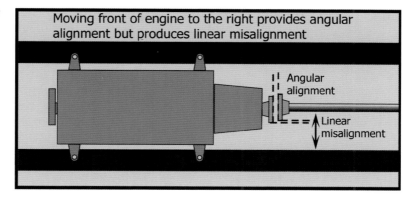

Moving front of engine to the right provides angular alignment but produces linear misalignment

Angular alignment

Linear misalignment

Initial correct alignment.

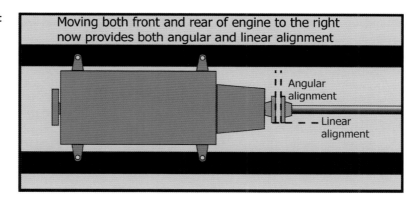

Moving both front and rear of engine to the right now provides both angular and linear alignment

Angular alignment

Linear alignment

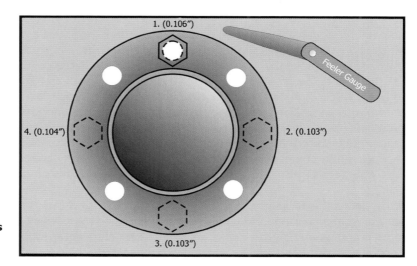

1. (0.106")

4. (0.104")

2. (0.103")

3. (0.103")

Feeler Gauge

Using feeler gauges to check the final angular alignment.

shorter component life. The same applies to linear alignment, in that if the couplings are bolted up with the engine and shaft out of alignment, the same stresses will again be set up.

The bolt holes for the engine feet can now be drilled and the fixing bolts loosely fitted so that final alignment of the gearbox coupling and shaft can be started. The final alignment is crucial to the success of the whole project and must be accurately performed. Although it requires care, it is no more complicated than the initial alignment and only requires patience and precise measurement. The alignment process should be carried out without the flexible coupling that will eventually fit between the gearbox and shaft. This ensures that the steel faces of the half couplings align perfectly before the less precise rubber or plastic flexible coupling is introduced.

Aligning the Half-Couplings

The gearbox half-coupling can now be aligned with the prop-shaft half-coupling. These couplings are machined with a matching spigot and aperture to ensure they mate perfectly, but to ensure they are properly aligned the mating faces must be kept apart until the alignment process is finished. It is possible (and quite easy) to let the two mating faces slip together while they are still misaligned, and although they will appear to be in alignment, the shaft may be forced into a slight curve that is invisible to the naked eye. The result will be shaft whip, vibration and early bearing failure. To ensure that this doesn't happen, the two mating faces are therefore aligned with the faces parted.

Athwartship and Vertical Alignment

Athwartship alignment is achieved by moving the engine and its mounts either left or right across the boat (using the transverse slotted bolt holes in the mounts), while vertical alignment is achieved using the adjusting nuts on the flexible mounts. However, as already stated, it is recommended that when using these adjusters the nuts should be as near to the bottom of the thread as possible to prevent excessive angular movement of the threaded studs under prop-shaft thrust. This makes it important to ensure that there is very little vertical misalignment before final adjustments are made. If it is found that the adjusting nuts are near the top of the thread it is better to place packing pieces beneath the feet to raise them to allow the adjusting nuts to be run further down the threads.

Linear and Angular Alignment of the Couplings

Linear and initial angular alignment must be checked at the same time, as one affects the other. Moving the back of the engine to bring the couplings into linear alignment generally means that the front will also need moving to maintain the angular alignment. By only moving the back an angular misalignment is introduced that must be checked and removed. The subsequent moving of the front of the engine then introduces another linear misalignment at the coupling. The process must be repeated until the couplings are in both linear and angular alignment. A steel straight-edge laid along the edge of both coupling flanges shows linear alignment; measuring the gap between the couplings provides initial angular alignment.

Accurate linear alignment must be completed at this stage, as once the couplings are bolted together it is impossible to check this aspect due to the flexibility of the propeller shaft which will always appear to be aligned when subsequently bolted up to the gearbox coupling.

Installing the Flexible Couplings

With the couplings approximately aligned, the propeller shaft can be slid back to allow the flexible coupling of whichever type to be installed between the two half-couplings. The basic coupling from R & D Marine provides some shock and vibration protection and is aligned using feeler gauges for the final checks.

There are six bolts to each half-coupling, one of which has a domed head to permit very accurate final angular alignment. The procedure is to turn the shaft until the domed head is at the 12 o'clock position, and the gap between the domed head and coupling face is then measured using feeler gauges. Make a note of the measurement, and turn the shaft so that the domed head is at the 6 o'clock position. Again measure the gap and make a note of the reading. Use the same procedure to measure the 3 o'clock and 9 o'clock positions; these last two should already read the same if the initial lining up was accurate.

The adjusting nuts on the flexible feet are then used to adjust the angle of the engine in conjunction with the shaft. Any athwartship angular misalignment must be removed by again moving the engine left or right by very small amounts. This can be achieved by slackening the holding-down bolts and lightly tapping the mounts in the required direction; this will usually be the front mounts, as these have the greatest effect on angular alignment. Tap the port mount and then tap the starboard mount the same number of times; this will result in the very small movements required to adjust the coupling alignment by a few thousands of an inch each time.

When the difference between the measured gap at each of the four positions is less than 5/1000in, the engine and shaft are satisfactorily aligned and the lock nuts on the mounts and mount securing bolts can be finally tightened. For wooden and lightly built GRP vessels it is essential to perform the final alignment when the vessel is afloat due to the inherent flexibility of the hull. In most relatively small steel vessels there is no hull flex, thanks to the enormous strength of their egg-box-like structures. Despite this it is good practice to check the alignment again once the vessel is afloat.

Completing the Fitting

With the engine accurately fitted, the parts that had been removed to allow it to pass through the roof hatch can be refitted. The gear and throttle cables can also be connected. With the engine finally sitting in position and bolted down in alignment with the shaft, the heavy work is complete.

CHAPTER 11

On-Board Tools and Spares

Self-sufficiency afloat is the essence of good seamanship, which means not only being able to understand a chart and handle rough weather conditions, it also, perhaps more importantly, means being able to cope with any breakdowns, whether major or minor, that occur while under way. To be able to do this requires not only an understanding of the engine, but also the right tools for the job, and the appropriate spares kit covering all the most likely items to fail in service.

THE TOOLKIT

If a power cruiser breaks down at sea it is generally the skipper who must rectify the problem and get the boat under way again to return to safety under its own power.

Any vessel that puts to sea, however small, should always have some means of auxiliary propulsion as back-up against unexpected breakdowns, whether it be a simple pair of oars for the smallest of dinghies, a small outboard motor on a swing-down bracket on medium-sized motor cruisers, an inboard wing engine on larger vessels, or of course twin engines on any size of craft. Sailing vessels are in the happy position that they have a set of sails to keep them going if the engine expires – and anyway in most cases only use the engine to enter and leave their moorings.

For powered craft, having some means of auxiliary propulsion ensures that when the worst does happen the vessel can continue under power without resorting to calls for help from outside sources. It is extremely selfish as well as very poor seamanship to go to sea relying on others to come to the rescue, and possibly risking their own lives, just because your vessel is not properly equipped.

However, even the best equipped and maintained craft can suffer from breakdowns at sea due to any number of unexpected causes, and although the back-up motor will keep the boat going (assuming that it hasn't also failed perhaps because of a common fuel fault), it will be at greatly reduced speed. There are few twin-engined craft that can maintain planing speed with one engine stopped, so at best the trip is slowed very considerably. Often the fault is quite minor and can be repaired in a few minutes if the correct tools are available, but if these have been left in the boot of the car (or worse still, in Halfords showroom) or are not comprehensive enough to cover all the various bolt-head sizes in common use, it is not only inconvenient but also extremely frustrating, especially if both engines are out of action and an RT call for help has to be made.

The problem with boat engines and equipment today is the differing nut and

A typical general toolkit that will handle the majority of minor problems.

bolt types used. 'Whitworth' sizes are still very common on old engines and mechanical gearboxes, stern gear and some American equipment, and 'AF' sizes were standard on most British engines up to thirty years ago, with many thousands still in service. Metric sizes have now taken over entirely on new European equipment.

This means that the average boat owner will need three sets of tools to cover all the bolt sizes likely to be encountered on their boat. Good quality socket sets usually have a selection of each type, but spanner sets need to be bought separately.

The following tools should make up the on-board toolkit:

The 'Metrinch 6WD' system: This system of sockets and spanners from Imperial Tools is quite revolutionary because they fit all types of nut or bolt head. For instance the 13mm socket or spanner will also fit the nearest-sized AF and Whitworth bolt, meaning that the set of tools can consist of only 30 per cent of the standard type while still covering the full range of sizes. They work on the flat of the bolt head rather than the corners, as is the case with the standard socket or spanner, and so avoid the problem of rounded-off corners on the bolt head, which often occurs with worn and ill-fitting spanners.

The design allows the tools to be a looser fit on the bolt heads than is normal with standard tools, and for experienced mechanics this takes some getting used to; but other than this these sets are ideal as a basis for the on-board toolkit because they reduce the overall number of tools required. Unfortunately they are very expensive, although still a very good investment.

Some years ago 'Richmond' tools brought out a reasonably priced 'Metrinch 6WD' socket and spanner set, but this is no longer produced. However, they do very occasionally come up on the second-hand market and are well worth buying.

Adjustable spanners: In any boat there is always the odd nut or bolt which is outside the range of the standard toolkit, and this is where a good quality adjustable spanner will often prove useful. In fact it is worth having a set of adjustables to cover all sizes, as they can be very useful when

A 'Metrinch' socket on the left; standard metric and imperial sockets to the right.

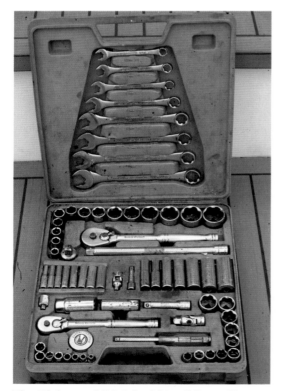

The Richmond 'Metrinch' toolkit, sadly no longer in production.

an additional spanner of a particular size is needed.

Small size spanners are also essential, especially when bleeding a fuel system, and a cheap socket set with very small sizes is also extremely useful for getting into awkward spots where the standard set cannot reach.

Pipe wrenches: A large 'Stilson' pipe wrench is yet another excellent multi-function tool in that it will adjust out to very large sizes to unscrew items such as stern glands or propeller nuts. Similarly the trusty 'mole' vice grip wrench, pliers, side cutters and long-nose pliers will all come in useful at some stage.

Hammers and screwdrivers: A selection of hammers is worth investing in, from a 2lb 'club' hammer to a light ball pein; they will always find a use. Equally a selection of screwdrivers is almost essential, including slot, Phillips and 'Posidrive' in a variety of sizes.

Allen keys: Hexagon-head 'Allen' keys are usually required at some stage, and sets can now be bought which fit into

A budget ¼in and ⅜in socket set is ideal for getting into tight spaces.

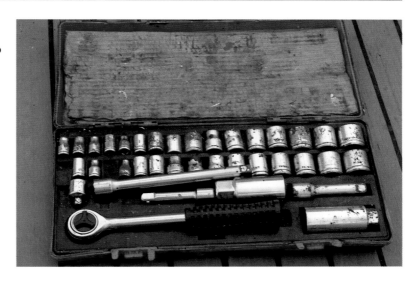

socket-set drives, making them very much more versatile. In recent years 'Torx' bolts have begun replacing Allen head bolts, so a set of these may also be required.

Hacksaws: A hacksaw and junior hacksaw have many uses and should be considered essential, while a 12-volt electrical soldering iron will make light electrical repairs a possibility, and a blowlamp, solder and flux will also increase the scope for plumbing and heavy electrical repairs.

Drill bits: A set of drill bits of all sizes is another essential, and it is also important to keep the set up to date – unlike the sad and depleted set pictured overleaf. So when a bit breaks, make a note to replace it as soon as possible (I'm off to the tool shop as soon as I've finished here!).

Sets of both metric and imperial Allen keys are essential.

Drill-bit sets need to be kept up to date, and breakages replaced.

Power tools: These are not generally required for emergency repairs, but a drill and small grinder come in very handy when small items such as brackets need to be made up.

Buying Tools

Buying tools is still very much a case of 'getting what you pay for', and it is often worth investing in the best possible set available – although it must be said that moderately priced socket sets will usually offer good service, as will spanners. However, it is worth paying a little extra for good quality screwdrivers, which will last without the points breaking or bending. Even so, I must admit that many Chinese tools are now of very good quality despite their low cost, and names such as Blackspur are worth considering.

The only practical method of ensuring that the toolset remains on the boat is to have a separate set of tools permanently on board. Although this can prove expensive when another set is required in the car, and a further set at home, it could turn out even more expensive if a particu-

An electric drill and mini grinder are often useful for fabricating small items.

lar tool needed for an emergency repair at sea were left in the garage at home!

The Toolbox

Once the tools have been purchased it is pointless to throw them into the bilges to rust away: they should be stored in a proper toolbox ready for immediate use. There are many good quality plastic boxes on the market at reasonable prices which are ideal for boat use, and if the tools are given an occasional spray with WD40 they will remain in good condition ready for immediate use when problems arise.

THE SPARES KIT

The on-board spares kit will vary from boat to boat, and there is no set kit to suit every need. When compiling the spares list for the boat, the first decision is how comprehensive the kit needs to be, and this will ultimately be decided by the length of the cruises that are envisaged and the ultimate destinations. For instance a boat venturing far abroad will require a more comprehensive kit than one that stays on the inland waterways or coast of Britain.

The obvious place to start compiling the kit is with the engine. Assuming the boat is remaining within the UK or the near Continent, it will not be necessary to carry such spares as pistons and valves, as a major breakdown involving items such as these will usually curtail the cruise and involve professional assistance.

However, items that suffer from fatigue and eventual failure such as raw water pump impellers, hoses and drive belts should be carried and stored ready for use. Self-amalgamating tape is ideal for making running repairs on split hoses on engine cooling pipes and other areas of the boat, so a large roll, available from chandlers, is worth carrying. Some marine engines require the water-pump pipework to be removed before a drive belt can be replaced, which makes an otherwise simple job rather more time-consuming. Nevertheless, it is often possible to tape a spare belt into place behind the pipework and out of the way of the running belt, so in an emergency it can be fitted quickly without removing the pipework.

Basic consumable spares consisting of belts, filters, fuses and water-pump impeller.

A spare raw water pump ready to fit can save a lot of time when at sea.

The following items should be included in the spares kit:

Impellers: Raw water pump impellers are another essential, but as mentioned previously, I strongly recommend carrying a complete spare pump ready to replace the complete unit in the event of impeller failure. This will avoid possible problems with the old pump not priming when the impeller has been changed, as can sometimes happen, and will also ensure that none of the small cover bolts are lost when changing the impeller in rough conditions.

Gasket set: A general gasket set for the engine is worth carrying should more extensive repairs be needed when back in port. A tube of instant gasket sealant will come in handy to cure oil leaks when the

A complete engine gasket set for more comprehensive repairs.

correct gasket is not on board, and also a roll of gasket paper so that gaskets can be fabricated on the spot. Most boats already have some polyurethane sealant such as Sikaflex on board, and this makes excellent emergency gaskets.

Fuel filters: A good supply of fuel filters is important, as a blocked fuel line caused by stirred-up sediment in the tank in rough weather will quickly stop a diesel engine. Some spare fuel-delivery tubing (usually copper) for replacing fractured pipework, and compression joints to cover every area of the fuel system, are essential if a reliable and permanent repair is to be made. A fuel lift pump overhaul kit including a replacement diaphragm is a good addition, although a complete spare pump is better as it can be changed in a matter of minutes in the (unlikely) event of sudden failure.

Injectors: A spare injector is a worthwhile item, because although a single faulty injector will not usually stop an engine, it will cause a loss of power and a smoky exhaust, and may lead to mechanical damage if allowed to drip fuel into the bore. Another essential is a set of spare injector pipes in case one should fracture. It may be possible to carry one long pipe and bend it into shape to suit the faulty pipe, but great care must be taken to ensure that the pipe is not weakened during bending, and for the price of a full set it is hardly worth taking the risk.

Lubricating oils: Naturally a plentiful supply of lubricating oils of the correct grade for engine and gearbox will also be needed, as well as more than sufficient fuel for the trip with a good margin for safety. Running out of fuel at sea indicates a total lack of forethought and planning and is the height of bad seamanship!

Fuses: The electrical system will need spare fuses of all sizes, plus a supply of wire of different gauge for emergency repairs in the case of damage or burning. As we have seen, proper crimp terminals make 100 per cent reliable joints, and these are available in complete kits with a selection of terminals and a crimping tool. Some insulating tape and electrician's flux-cored solder will often come in handy as well. Another useful addition to the electrical spares is an alternator already fitted with the correct pulley to suit the engine.

Every owner will have their own additions to the list, and the items mentioned are by no means comprehensive, but they should form the basis of the spares kit, which can be extended to cover the needs of the individual boat depending on where it is cruising, how far and for how long.

An alternator ready to fit with the correct pulley already fitted.

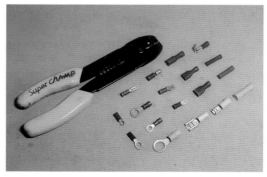

A selection of crimp terminals will always come in useful for both temporary repairs and permanent alterations.

SUGGESTED MINIMUM SPARES LIST

Fuel filters
Oil filters
Water pump impeller (or spare complete water pump)
Drive belts for alternator, water pump, etc
Copper tube, selection of sizes
Seal rings (olives), selection of sizes
Hoses, various sizes
Hose clips, various sizes
Self-amalgamating tape
Quick-cure epoxy
Nuts, bolts, washers, screws – various types and sizes
Water-repellent spray (WD40)
Engine starting fluid (Easy Start)
Electrical crimp terminals, all types

COMPREHENSIVE ON-BOARD TOOLKIT

Socket set – AF, metric and Whitworth sizes (or 'Metrinch')
Spanners, open-ended and ring – AF, metric and Whitworth sizes (or 'Metrinch')
'Stilson' pipe-wrench – Large
Adjustable spanners – Small, medium and large
Vice grip wrench – ('Mole' type)
Pliers – Standard and long-nose
Side cutters
'Allen' keys – Imperial and metric
'Torx' keys
Screwdrivers – Slot, Phillips and Posidrive
Hammers – 2lb club and light ball pein
Hacksaws – Standard and junior
Blowlamp
Jabsco impeller removing tool
Electrical connection crimp tool
12-volt electrical soldering iron
Heavy duty plastic toolbox

Glossary

After-cooler Similar in design to a heat exchanger, the after- (or inter-) cooler cools and condenses the compressed intake air provided by a turbocharger or supercharger and further boosts power output.

Agglomerator A fine fuel filter that collects tiny drops of water and combines them until they are large enough to sink to the bottom of the filter body for draining.

Arc welding A process involving flux-coated metal rods that melt and fuse with other metals when brought into close proximity so that an electric arc is formed due to the current supplied by the transformer. The flux coating forms a gas as the rod melts and excludes oxygen from the welded joint to prevent the metals becoming brittle.

Calorifier A domestic water storage tank with a heating coil within, which is fed with hot water from the fresh cooling system of the engine, providing free hot water from waste heat produced by the engine.

Camshaft Running at half engine speed, the camshaft operates the opening and closing of the inlet and exhaust valves.

Common rail A diesel fuel reservoir supplying fuel at injection pressure to the injectors of modern, electronically controlled diesel engines.

Compression joint A mechanical joint used in pipework to provide a perfect seal which can be opened and resealed many times without losing the effectiveness of the seal.

Core plug A plug fitted into the outer water jacket of an engine block, designed to push out under the pressure of ice when the engine has frozen due to lack of anti-freeze to prevent the block from cracking.

Crankshaft The component that converts the up/down movement of the pistons into the rotary motion of the output shaft.

Crimp terminal A cable end fitting that provides the means of making a professional quality joint. Available in a variety of sizes and styles to suit different applications. Low cost kits complete with crimping tool are available from car accessory shops.

Direct injection A term used to describe engines where the fuel is sprayed directly on top of the piston.

Direct cooling A method of water cooling where the water from the river or sea is pumped directly around the engine block before being expelled, usually via the exhaust.

External combustion The process of producing heat energy from an external source away from the cylinder of an engine, resulting in massive heat loss and minimal efficiency. Used in steam engines.

Four-stroke cycle A series of four strokes of a piston, two up and two down, which form the complete combustion cycle of a four-stroke engine, requiring two revolutions of the crankshaft.

Fuel lift pump A mechanically operated pump, driven from the camshaft, which lifts fuel from the tank and passes it into the fuel system via the filters.

Gas-oil The standard fuel for diesel engines, with a higher flash point than petrol, which almost eradicates the risk of explosion, making it highly suitable for marine use.

Heater plugs Cold start devices incorporating a heating coil and which are screwed into every combustion chamber of the engine to warm the air within and assist with cold starting.

Hot bulb engine A design of internal combustion engine developed and commercially produced by Herbert Akroyd Stuart, which many people consider to be the first real diesel engine and often referred to as a 'semi-diesel'.

Impeller The moving part of a rotary pump which moves the liquid. It may be made of metal or a flexible material such as the rubber or nitrile used in Jabsco raw water pumps.

Indirect injection A term used to describe engines with pre-combustion chambers.

Indirect cooling A method of water cooling where the water from the river or sea passes through tubes in a heat exchanger, which transfers the heat from the fresh water circulating through the block.

Injection pump Meters the amount of fuel to be sprayed into the cylinder at any given throttle setting and the time of injection on the combustion cycle.

Injector Also referred to as an atomizer. A self-sealing valve that atomizes a precise metered amount of fuel and sprays it into the combustion chamber under pressure from the injection pump.

Internal combustion The process of producing heat energy from fuel within the cylinder of an engine, which reduces heat loss and provides maximum efficiency from the burned fuel. Used in diesel and petrol engines.

Master spline The large spline on an injection pump drive spindle which ensures that the spindle can only be inserted into the drive in the correct alignment.

Mig welding Works on the same electrical principle as the arc welder, but uses continuous flexible wire fed from a motor-driven drum in place of rods, and a canister of inert gas to exclude oxygen from the joint in place of flux.

Olive A metal ring, usually of brass or copper, used to seal a compression pipe-joint.

Piston ring A split ring that fits in a groove in the wall of a piston and forms a seal against the cylinder wall.

Power-to-weight ratio The output power of an engine compared to its weight. A heavy engine with a low power output would have a lower power-to-weight ratio than a lightweight unit with a high power output.

Pre-combustion chamber A small chamber off the main cylinder where fuel is sprayed in at the ignition point, and which offers smoother running at the cost of slightly reduced fuel economy.

Raw water pump Used to draw water from the river or sea for engine cooling; may be used in both direct and indirect cooled systems.

Sedimenter A coarse filter used to remove large quantities of water and dirt from fuel before the fuel enters the fine filter.

Spark plug An electrical igniter used to assist the combustion process within petrol engines.

Sump The oil reservoir at the bottom of the engine, usually a pressed steel fabrication.

Supercharger Also known as a compressor on certain foreign cars and engines. A belt- or chain-driven air pump that provides forced induction at low revs to provide additional torque and acceleration to help sports cruisers achieve planing speed more quickly.

Thermostart A cold start device mounted in the inlet manifold, utilizing a heating coil that opens a fuel valve to allow fuel on to the coil. The fuel is ignited and the flames are drawn into the cylinders to assist with cold starting.

Turbocharger A turbine-powered air pump driven by exhaust gases which raises the intake pressure to provide greater power output.

Two-stroke cycle A series of two strokes of a piston, one up and one down, which forms the complete combustion cycle of a two-stroke engine, requiring one revolution of the crankshaft.

Voltage drop The difference between voltage measured at a battery and at the end of a long section of cable.

Useful Contacts

Lancing Marine
51 Victoria Road
Portslade
East Sussex
BN41 1XY
Tel: 01273 411765
Email: data@lancingmarine.com
www.lancingmarine.com

Marinizing specialist

ASAP Supplies Ltd
Reed House
Ellough Industrial Estate
Beccles
Suffolk
NR34 7TD
Tel: 0845 1300 870
Email: email@asap-supplies.com
www.asap-supplies.com

Marinizing equipment, engine spares and all general boat equipment

Halyard (Marine & Industrial) Limited
Whaddon Business Park
Southampton Road
Whaddon
Salisbury
SP5 3HF
Tel: 01722 710922
Email: jgrazebrook@halyard.eu.com
www.halyard.eu.com

Drive couplings, exhaust systems, engine mounts and sound proofing

CENTA Transmissions Ltd.
Thackley Court
Thackley Old Road
Shipley
Bradford
West Yorkshire
BD18 1BW
Tel: 01274 531034
Email: sales@centa-uk.co.uk
www.centa-uk.co.uk

Drive couplings

R&D Marine Ltd.
Meadow Works,
Clothall Road,
Baldock,
Herts.SG7 6PD
Tel: 01462 892391
Email: info@randdmarine.com
www.randdmarine.co.uk

Drive couplings

Index Marine Equipment Ltd
Unit 5 Cortry Close,
Branksome Business Park,
Poole,
Dorset.BH12 4BQ
Tel: 01202-746000
Email: sales@marineelectrics.co.uk
www.marineelectrics.co.uk

Marine electrical equipment, wiring and switches

Index